The Wisdom of
FREUD

The Wisdom of

FREUD

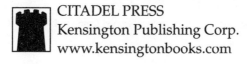

CITADEL PRESS
Kensington Publishing Corp.
www.kensingtonbooks.com

Grateful acknowledgment and thanks is expressed to the publishers and owners of copyrights listed below for their kind permission to quote copyrighted material from the following books and papers by Dr. Sigmund Freud:

George Allen & Unwin Ltd., London, England, publisher of *The Interpretation of Dreams.*
Ernest Benn Ltd., London, England, publisher of *Psychopathology of Everyday Life.*
Mrs. A.A. Brill, New York, N. Y., owner of copyright of *Totem and Taboo* and *Wit and Its Relation to the Unconscious.*
Dodd, Mead & Co., New York, N. Y., American publisher of *Totem and Taboo* and *Wit and Its Relation to the Unconscious.*
The Hogarth Press Ltd., London, England, publisher of *An Autobiographical Study, Civilization and Its Discontents, Collected Papers (Vols. I–V), Beyond the Pleasure Principle, The Ego and the Id, Group Psychology and the Analysis of the Ego.*
Alfred Knopf, Inc., New York, N. Y., publisher of *Moses and Monotheism.*
Nervous and Mental Disease Monographs, New York, N. Y., publisher of *Three Contributions to the Theory of Sex.*
W.W. Norton & Co., Inc., New York, N. Y., publisher of *New Introductory Lectures on Psychoanalysis, An Outline of Psychoanalysis, The Problem of Anxiety, The Question of Lay Analysis* (quotations by permission of W. W. Norton & Co., Inc., copyright, 1933, by Sigmund Freud, 1936, by The Psychoanalytical Quarterly, Inc., 1949, 1950, by W. W. Norton & Co., Inc.)
Random House, Inc., New York, N. Y., publisher of *Leonardo da Vinci—A Study in Psychosexuality* and *The Basic Writings of Sigmund Freud.*
Routledge & Kegan Paul Ltd., London, England, British publisher of *Totem and Taboo* and *Wit and Its Relation to the Unconscious.*

CITADEL PRESS books are published by

Kensington Publishing Corp.
850 Third Avenue
New York, NY 10022

Copyright © 1950 Philosophical Library, Inc.

First Citadel printing January 2002

10 9 8 7 6 5 4 3 2 1

Printed in the United States of America

Cataloging data for this title may be obtained from the Library of Congress.

ISBN 0-8065-2327-1

A

ABSTINENCE, SEXUAL—In considering the question of abstinence, far too little distinction is made between two forms of it, namely, abstention from any kind of sexual activity at all, and abstention from heterosexual intercourse.
CSMN

ADAPTABILITY, CULTURAL—A man's personal capacity for transformation of the egoistic impulses under the influence of the erotic.
TTWD

AFFECTIVITY—Affectivity manifests itself essentially in motor (*i.e.* secretory and circulatory) discharge resulting in an (internal) alteration of the subject's own body without reference to the outer world.
Ucs

AGGRESSION—The tendency to aggression is an innate, independent, instinctual disposition in man.
C & D—ch. 6
  When the superego begins to be formed, considerable

amounts of the aggressive instinct become fixated within the ego and operate there in a self-destructive fashion.
OoPA—ch. 2

The holding back of aggressiveness is in general unhealthy and leads to illness.
OoPA—ch. 2

AGORAPHOBIA—The sufferer from agoraphobia imposes a restriction upon his ego in order to escape an instinctual danger. The instinctual danger in question is the temptation to yield to his erotic desires; and to yield to them would be to reincarnate once again, as in childhood, the specter of the danger of castration or of an analogous danger. As an example I may refer to the case of a young man who became agoraphobic because he was afraid of yielding to the allurements of prostitutes and of acquiring syphilis as a punishment. The symptomatology of agoraphobia is complicated by the fact that the ego is not content with renouncing something; in addition to this, it takes steps to deprive the situation of its danger. This additional measure is usually a regression to childhood (in extreme cases, to the uterus, to a period when one was protected against the dangers which threaten today); the regression constitutes the condition under which the renunciation need not be made. Thus the agoraphobic may go on the street provided that, like a small child, he is accompanied by a person in whom he has full confidence. A similar caution may also permit him to go out alone, provided that he does not go more than a certain distance away from home, that he does not enter localities which he does not know well and where the people do not know him. In the choice of these specifications there becomes manifest the influence of the infantile motives which govern him.
PoA—ch. 7

AMBITION—A . . . connection is to be found between ambition and urethral erotism.
NILP—ch. 4

AMBIVALENCE—This form of the sexual organization can already maintain itself throughout life and draws to itself a large part of sexual activity. The dominance of sadism and the rôle of the cloaca of the anal zone stamps it with an exquisitely archaic impression. As another characteristic belonging to it, we can mention the fact that the contrasting pair of impulses are developed in almost the same manner, a situation which was happily designated by Bleuler by the term *ambivalence*.
TCTS II

AMNESIA

Amnesia, Hysterical—In hysteria it is possible for a traumatic impression to become subjected to amnesia.
PoA—ch. 6

Amnesia, Infantile—The peculiar amnesia which veils from most people (not from all) the first years of their childhood, usually the first six or eight years.
TCTS II
  With few exceptions, the events of the early period of sexuality fall a victim to *infantile amnesia*.
OoPA—ch. 3
  I believe we accept too indifferently the fact of *infantile amnesia*—that is, the failure of memory for the first years of our lives—and fail to find in it a strange riddle.
PEL—ch. 4
  The period of *infantile amnesia* coincides with this early blossoming of sexuality.
M & M—Part III, Section I

The period of infantile amnesia is often interrupted by isolated fragmentary memories, the so-called "screen-memories."
M & M—Part III, Section I

ANALYSIS [cf. also PSYCHOANALYSIS]—When in analysis we render the ego assistance enabling it to undo its repressions, the ego regains its power over the repressed id and can so steer the course of the instinctual impulses as if the old danger situation no longer existed. What we achieve in this way is in complete harmony with what we accomplish in other spheres of medical activity. As a rule our treatment has to be satisfied with bringing about more rapidly, more certainly and with less trouble the satisfactory outcome which under favorable conditions would have resulted spontaneously.
PoA—ch. 10
Analysis is built on complete frankness.
QLA—ch. 4

Analysis of Children—Naturally one has to make extensive alterations in the technique of treatment which has been developed for adults when one is dealing with children. The child is, psychologically, a different thing from the adult; it does not yet possess a super-ego, it cannot make much use of the method of free association, and transference plays a different part with it, since its real parents are still there. The internal resistances, against which we have to fight in the case of adults, are in the case of children for the most part replaced by external difficulties.
NILP—ch. 6

Analysis, Fundamental Rule of—We impose upon him [the neurotic] the *fundamental rule* of analysis, which is henceforward to govern his behavior to us. He must tell us not only what he can say intentionally and willingly, what will give him relief like a confession, but everything else besides that his self-observation presents him with— everything that comes into his head, even if it is *disagreeable* to say it, even if it seems *unimportant* or positively *meaningless*. OoPA—ch. 6

Analysis, Technique of—An analysis must go back to the patient's early childhood, because it was then, while the Ego was weak, that the decisive repressions occurred. QLA—ch. 4

A correct reconstruction of such forgotten childhood experiences always has great therapeutic effects, whether it can also be confirmed from outside sources or not. QLA—ch. 4

We induce the thus enfeebled [neurotic] ego to take part in the purely intellectual work of interpretation, which aims at provisionally filling the gaps in his mental resources, and to transfer to us the authority of his superego; we stimulate his ego to take up the struggle over each individual demand made by the id and to defeat the resistances which arise in connection with it. At the same time, we restore order in his ego, by detecting the material and impulses which have forced their way in from the unconscious, and expose them to criticism by tracing them back to their origin. OoPA—ch. 6

The analyst never encourages the patient into the sexual field, he does not say in advance, "We must deal with the intimacies of your sexual life"! He lets him begin his communications where he likes, waiting quietly until he himself touches on sexual matters. QLA—ch. 4

Analysis, dreams in the—The analyst links up the communication which he has received in the form of a dream with the patient's other communications and proceeds with the analysis.
NILP—ch. 1

Analysis, technique of—In civilian life illness may be used as a protection—to palliate incapacity at work or among competitors, or in family life as a means to force sacrifices and demonstrations of affection from others, or impose one's will upon them. All this is comparatively on the surface, and we put it all together under the heading "advantage gained by illness"; the only remarkable thing is that the patient—his Ego—knows nothing of the whole connection of such motives with his resulting behavior. One combats the influence of these impulses by forcing the Ego to accept this knowledge.
QLA—ch. 5

ANALYST—No one should practice analysis who has not qualified himself by a proper training. Whether the person is a doctor or not seems to me of altogether minor importance.
QLA—ch. 5

Analyst, personal influence of—Such an influence does exist, and plays a big part in the analysis. We do not employ this personal influence—the "suggestive" element—to suppress the symptoms from which the patient suffers, as is done in hypnotic suggestion. Further, it would be a mistake to think that this element bears the brunt and provides the main furtherance in the treatment. At first, yes; but later it stands in the way of our analytical purposes, and forces us to take most extensive countermeasures.
QLA—ch. 1

The neurotic sets himself to the work because he believes in the analyst, and he believes in him because he begins to entertain certain feelings towards him. The attitude is, in fact—to put it bluntly—a kind of falling in love. The patient *repeats*, in the form of falling in love with the analyst, psychical experiences which he underwent before; he has *transferred* to the analyst psychical attitudes which lay ready within him, and which were intimately linked with the inception of his neurosis. He repeats, too, his onetime defense reactions before our eyes, and wants nothing so much as to repeat all the vicissitudes of that forgotten period in his relations with the analyst. So what he is showing us is the very core of his most private life; *he is palpably reproducing it, as though it were all happening in the present, instead of remembering it.* With this, the riddle of transference-love is solved, and with the very help of the new situation, which seemed so threatening, the analysis can make progress.
QLA—ch. 5

ANXIETY—Anxiety is in the first place something felt. We call it an affective state, although we are equally ignorant of what an affect is. As a feeling it is of most obviously unpleasurable character, but this is not by any means a complete description of its quality; not every state of unpleasure may we call anxiety.

The analysis of the anxiety state gives us as its attributes: (1) a specific unpleasurable quality, (2) efferent or discharge phenomena, and (3) the perception of these.
PoA—ch. 8

Anxiety is a specific state of unpleasure accompanied by motor discharge along definite pathways.
PoA—ch. 8

Anxiety is the reaction to the danger of object loss.
PoA—ch. 11

8 THE WISDOM OF FREUD

The psychology of the neuroses taught us that when wish feelings undergo repression their libido becomes transformed into anxiety.
T & T—ch. 2

When the ego is forced to acknowledge its weakness, it breaks out into anxiety: reality anxiety in face of the external world, normal anxiety in face of the super-ego, and neurotic anxiety in face of the strength of the passions in the id.
NILP—ch. 3

The ego withdraws (preconscious) cathexis from the instinct representative which is to be repressed and utilizes it in the release of unpleasure (anxiety).
PoA—ch. 2

We have no reason to ascribe any expression of anxiety to the superego. Anxiety is an affective state which can of course be experienced only by the ego. The id cannot be afraid, as the ego can; it is not an organization, and cannot estimate situations of danger.
PoA—ch 8

Anxiety is after all only a perception—of possibilities of anxiety.
C & D—ch. 8

Anxiety, Neurotic—Neurotic anxiety is anxiety in regard to a danger which we do not know.
PoA—ch. 11

In a little essay on *Anxiety Neurosis*, written in 1895, I maintain that neurotic anxiety has its origin in the sexual life, and corresponds to a libido which has been deflected from its object and has found no employment. The accuracy of this formula has since then been demonstrated with ever-increasing certainty. From it we may deduce the doctrine that anxiety-dreams are dreams of sexual content, and that

the libido appertaining to this content has been transformed into anxiety.
IoD—ch. 4

Anxiety, Object of—Let us call such a [danger] situation in which the efforts of the pleasure-principle come to nothing, a "traumatic" factor; in that way, by following the series, neurotic anxiety—objective anxiety—danger-situation, we can arrive at a simple formula: what is feared, the object of the anxiety, is always the emergence of a traumatic factor, which cannot be dealt with in accordance with the norms of the pleasure-principle.
NILP—ch. 4

Anxiety and Repression—It may still be correct to say that in repression anxiety is created out of the libidinal cathexis of instinctual impulses.
PoA—ch. 4

Anxiety, Reproduction of—Anxiety arose as a response to a situation of *danger;* it will be regularly reproduced thenceforward whenever such a situation recurs.
PoA—ch. 8

Anxiety, Sexual Practices and—I found that certain sexual practices, such as coitus interruptus, frustrated excitement, enforced abstinence, give rise to outbreaks of anxiety and a general predisposition to anxiety—which may be induced whenever, therefore, sexual excitation is inhibited, frustrated or diverted in the course of its discharge in gratification.
PoA—ch. 4

Anxiety, Signal of—An increase in unpleasure which is expected and foreseen is met by a *signal of anxiety;* the occasion of this increase, whether it threatens from without or within, is called a *danger.*
OoPA—ch. 1

Anxiety, True (Real) and Neurotic—A real danger is a danger which we know, a true anxiety the anxiety in regard to such a known danger. Neurotic anxiety is anxiety in regard to a danger which we do not know. . . . There are cases in which the attributes of true and of neurotic anxiety are intermingled. The danger is known and of the real type, but the anxiety in regard to it is disproportionately great, greater than in our judgment it ought to be. It is by this excess that the neurotic element stands revealed.
PoA—ch. 11

ART—Incomplete and dim memories of the past, which we call tradition, are a great incentive to the artist, for he is free to fill in the gaps in the memories according to the behests of his imagination and to form after his own purpose the image of the time he has undertaken to reproduce.
M & M—Part III, Section I

As artistic talent and productive ability are intimately connected with sublimation, we have to admit also that the nature of artistic attainment is psychoanalytically inaccessible to us.
LDV—ch. 6

ASSOCIATIONS—Whenever one psychic element is connected with another by an obnoxious and superficial association, there exists also a correct and more profound connection between the two, which succumbs to the resistance of the censorship.
IoD—ch. 7

Associations in Dream Interpretation—Although in dream interpretation we are in general and predominantly dependent on the associations of the dreamer, nevertheless we treat certain elements of the content quite independently— mainly because we have to, because as a rule, associations refuse to come.

NILP—ch. 1

The associations to the dream are not the latent dreamthoughts. They are contained, but not completely contained, in the associations.

NILP—ch. 1

AUTOEROTISM—The most striking character of this sexual activity is that the impulse is not directed to other persons but that the child gratifies himself on his own body; to use the happy term invented by Havelock Ellis, we will say that he is *autoerotic*.

TCTS II

B

BEAUTY—Beauty is an instance which plainly shows that culture is not simply utilitarian in its aims, for the lack of beauty is a thing we cannot tolerate in civilization.
C & D—ch. 3

BED-WETTING—We are inclined to adopt the simple generalization that continued bed-wetting is a result of masturbation and that its suppression is regarded by boys as an inhibition of their genital activity, that is, as having the meaning of a threat of castration; but whether we are always right in supposing this remains to be seen.
AnDS

BEHEADING—Certain patients suffering from obsessions treat being beheaded as a substitute for being castrated.
C-S & S

BIOLOGY—The impulses and their transformations are the last things psychoanalysis can discern. Henceforth it leaves the stage to biological investigation. . . . Biological investigation of our time endeavors to explain the chief traits of the organic constitution of a person through the fu-

sion of male and female predispositions in the material sense.
LDV—ch. 6

BISEXUALITY—Man, too, is an animal with an unmistakably bisexual disposition. The individual represents a fusion of two symmetrical halves, of which, according to many authorities, one is purely male, the other female.
C & D—ch. 4

Parts of the male sexual apparatus are also to be found in the body of the female, although in a rudimentary condition, and *vice versa*. Science sees in this phenomenon an indication of *bi-sexuality*, as though the individual were neither man nor woman, but both at the same time, only rather more the one than the other.
NILP—ch 5

For the purpose of distinguishing between male and female in mental life we assert an equivalence which is clearly insufficient, empirical and conventional: we call everything that is powerful and active "male" and everything that is weak and passive "female."
OoPA—ch. 7

C

CASTRATION ANXIETY (FEAR, COMPLEX)—A male child commonly suffers from anxiety lest his father rob him of his male member; and so castration anxiety is one of the strongest influences on the development of his character, and decisive for his sexual tendencies later.
QLA—ch. 4

Before the child came under the domination of the castration complex, at the time when he still held the woman at her full value, he began to manifest an intensive desire to look, as an erotic activity of his impulse. He wished to see the genitals of other persons, originally probably because he wished to compare them with his own. The erotic attraction which emanated from the person of his mother soon reached its height in the longing to see her genital, which he believed to be a penis. With the cognition acquired only later that the woman has no penis, this longing often becomes transformed into its opposite and gives place to disgust, which in the years of puberty may become the cause of psychic impotence, of misogyny and of lasting homosexuality. But the fixation on the once so vividly desired object, the penis of the woman, leaves ineradicable traces in the psychic life of the child, which has gone through that frag-

ment of infantile sexual investigation with particular thoroughness. The fetish-like reverence for the feminine foot and shoe seems to take the foot only as a substitutive symbol for the once revered and since then missed member of the woman. The "braid-snippers," without knowing it, play the part of persons who perform the act of castration on the female genital.
LDV—ch. 3

CHARACTER—What we call the *character* of the person is built up to a large extent from the material of sexual excitations; it is composed of impulses fixed since infancy and won through sublimation, and of such structures as are destined to suppress effectually those perverse feelings which are recognized as useless.
TCTS III

CHILD—A more searching investigation into the psychic life of the child teaches us, of course, that sexual motives, in infantile forms, play a very considerable part, which has been too long overlooked, in the psychic activity of the child. This permits us to doubt to some extent the happiness of the child, as imagined later by adults.
IoD—ch. 3

The child is long before puberty a being capable of mature love, lacking only the ability for reproduction.
SECh

Girls—A comparison with what happens in the case of the boy shows us that the development of the little girl into a normal woman is more difficult and more complicated.
NILP—ch. 5

The little girl is as a rule less aggressive, less defiant, and less self-sufficient; she seems to have a greater need for af-

fection to be shown her, and therefore to be more dependent and docile. . . . One gets the impression, too, that the
little girl is more intelligent and more lively than the boy of
the same age; she is more inclined to meet the external
world half way, and, at the same time, she makes stronger
object-cathexes.
NILP—ch. 4

Children, Amorality of—Small children are notoriously
amoral. They have no internal inhibitions against their
pleasure-seeking impulses.
NILP—ch. 3

Child, Attitude to Brothers and Sisters—A child is absolutely egotistical; he feels his wants acutely, and strives
remorselessly to satisfy them, especially against his competitors, other children, and first of all against his brothers
and sisters. . . . I seriously declare it as my opinion that a
child is able to estimate the disadvantages which he has to
expect on account of a new-comer.
IoD—ch 5

CHILD PSYCHOLOGY—Child psychology, in my opinion, is destined to render the same services to the psychology of adults as a study of the structure or development of
the lower animals renders to the investigation of the structure of the higher orders of animals.
IoD—ch. 3

CHILDHOOD

Childhood Experiences—The psychoanalyses of individuals have taught us that their earliest impressions, received
at a time when they were hardly able to talk, manifest them-

selves later in an obsessive fashion, although those impressions themselves are not consciously remembered.
M & M—Part III, Section II

The experience of the first five years of childhood exerts a decisive influence on our life, one which later events oppose in vain. . . . The strongest obsessive influence derives from those experiences which the child undergoes at a time when we have reason to believe his physical apparatus to be incompletely fitted for accepting them. . . . What a child has experienced and not understood by the time he has reached the age of two he may never again remember, except in his dreams. Only through psychoanalytic treatment will he become aware of those events. At any time in later years, however, they may break into his life with obsessive impulsiveness, direct his actions, force him to like or dislike people, and often decide the choice of his love-object by a preference that so often cannot be rationally defended.
M & M—Part III, Section II

Childhood, Sexuality in—It seems certain that the newborn child brings with it the germs of sexual feelings which continue to develop for some time and then succumb to a progressive suppression, which may in turn be broken through by the regular advances of the sexual development or may be checked by individual idiosyncrasies. Nothing is known concerning the laws and periodicity of this oscillating course of development. It seems, however, that the sexual life of the child mostly manifests itself in the third or fourth year in some form accessible to observation.
TCTS II

The first period of childhood, during which the ego begins to be differentiated from the id, is also the period of early sexual efflorescence which is brought to an end by the period of latency; it can hardly be a matter of chance that

this momentous early period subsequently falls a victim to infantile amnesia, and finally that biological modifications in sexual life (such as its diphasic onset to which we have just referred, the disappearance of the periodic character of sexual excitement and the transformation in the relation between female menstruation and male excitation)—that these innovations in sexuality must have been of high importance in the evolution of animals into men.
OoPA—ch. 7

CLOTHING—Covering of the body, which keeps abreast with civilization, continuously arouses sexual curiosity and serves to supplement the sexual object by uncovering the hidden parts.
TCTS I

COMPULSION NEUROSIS—The symptoms of compulsion neurosis are, broadly speaking, of two kinds and of contradictory purport. Either they are prohibitions or prophylactic measures or atonements, and are thus of a negative character, or they are on the other hand substitute gratifications, very often symbolic in disguise. The situation of origin in the case of compulsion neurosis is in fact none other than that in hysteria, namely, the defense necessary against the libidinal demands of the œdipus complex. Furthermore there seems to be present in every compulsion neurosis a lowermost layer of hysterical symptoms of very early formation. Its subsequent form, however, is then decisively altered by a constitutional factor.
PoA—ch. 5

Puberty forms a definite epoch in the development of the compulsion neurosis.
PoA—ch. 5

Perhaps in compulsion neurosis, even more clearly than

in normal and hysterical cases, we may recognize the castration complex as the motivating force of defense, the strivings of the œdipus complex as that which is defended against.
PoA—ch. 5

. . . it is precisely the suppressed onanism which in the form of compulsive acts compels an ever furthered approximation to gratification.
PoA—ch. 5

COMPULSIVE ACTS—A great many compulsive acts plainly serve as a precaution and an assurance against sexual experience and are therefore phobic in their character.
PoA—ch. 1

COMPULSIVE CEREMONIALS—Compulsive ceremonials have the intention to "undo" as their second root, their first being to prevent or to forestall some specific thing happening or being repeated. The distinction is easy enough to grasp; precautionary measures are of a rational character, "voiding" or "cancelling" by means of "undoing" of an irrational magical nature.
PoA—ch. 6

CONCENTRATION—Even in normal persons concentration is utilized to keep at a distance not solely matters of indifference, things that are irrelevant, but in particular things which run inconveniently counter to the matter in hand.
PoA—ch. 6

CONFESSION AND ANALYSIS—Confession enters into analysis, as its introduction, as it were. But it is far from being the same thing as analysis, and it cannot serve to explain its effect. In confession the sinner tells what he knows,

in analysis the neurotic must tell more. Besides, we have no knowledge that the system of confession has developed the power to get rid of direct symptoms of illness.
QLA—ch. 1

CONSCIENCE—Conscience is the inner perception of objections to definite wish impulses that exist in us; but the emphasis is put upon the fact that this rejection does not have to depend on anything else, that it is sure of itself. This becomes even plainer in the case of a guilty conscience, where we become aware of the inner condemnation of such acts which realized some of our definite wish impulses.
T & T—ch. 2

Conscience is a function we ascribe, among others, to the super-ego; it consists of watching over and judging the actions and intentions of the ego, exercising the functions of a censor.
C & D—ch. 8

The Super-Ego is the vehicle for the phenomenon we call "conscience."
QLA—ch. 5

CONSCIOUS, CONSCIOUSNESS—Being conscious is an ephemeral quality which adheres to a psychical process only temporarily.
M & M—Part III, Section I

One property of mental life, which may co-exist along with its other properties or may be absent.
E & I—ch. 1

For us the state of becoming conscious is a special psychic act, different from and independent of the process of becoming fixed or represented, and consciousness appears to us as a sensory organ which perceives a content proceeding from another source. It may be shown that psy-

chopathology simply cannot dispense with these fundamental assumptions.
IoD—ch. 4

It is a complicated matter for a psychical process to become conscious.
QLA—ch. 2

CRIMINAL MIND—I must work out an analogy between
the criminal and the hysteric. In both we are concerned
with a secret, with something hidden . . . In the case of the
criminal it is a secret which he knows and hides from you,
but in the case of the hysteric it is a secret hidden from him,
a secret he himself does not know.
PA & CL

CULTURE—The word "culture" describes the sum of the
achievements and institutions which differentiate our lives
from those of our animal forebears and serve two purposes,
namely, that of protecting humanity against nature and of
regulating the relations of human beings among themselves.
C & D—ch. 3

The cultural process is the particular modification undergone by the life-process under the influence of the task set
before it by Eros and stimulated by Ananke, external necessity.
C & D—ch. 8

D

DANGER—An increase in unpleasure which is expected and foreseen is met by a *signal of anxiety;* the occasion of this increase, whether it threatens from without or within, is called a *danger.*
OoPA—ch. 1
 In relation to the traumatic situation, against which one is helpless, external and internal danger, reality danger and instinctual demand, coincide.
PoA—ch. 11

DEFENSE (DEFENSIVE) MECHANISM—From the very outset the ego has to try to fulfil its task of acting as an intermediary between the id and the external world in the service of the pleasure principle, to protect the id from the dangers of the external world . . . In this battle on two fronts . . . the ego makes use of various methods of fulfilling its task, i.e. to put it in general terms, of avoiding danger, anxiety and unpleasure. We call these devices *defensive mechanisms.*
AT & I

DEGENERATION—The term, *degeneration,* is open to the objections which may be urged against the promiscuous use of this particular term. It has, in fact, become customary to designate all morbid manifestations not of traumatic or infectious origin as degenerative. It would seem more appropriate not to speak of degeneration: (1) where there are not many marked deviations from the normal; (2) where the capacity for working and living do not in general appear markedly impaired.

TCTS I

DENIAL—If we wish to differentiate between what happens to the *idea* as distinct from the *affect*, we can restrict "repression" to relate to the affect; the correct word for what happens to the idea is then "denial."

Fet

DELUSION—It has long been recognized that delusions contain a piece of forgotten truth, which had at its return to put up with being distorted and misunderstood, and that the compulsive conviction appertaining to the delusion emanates from this core of truth and spreads to the errors that enshroud it.

M & M—Part III, Section I

Delusion of Observation—One group of them [psychotics] suffer what we call delusions of observation. They complain to us that they suffer continually, and in their most intimate actions, from the observation of unknown powers or persons, and they have hallucinations in which they hear these persons announcing the results of their observations: "now he is going to say this, now he is dressing himself to go out," and so on. Such observation is not the same as persecution, but it is not far removed from it.

NILP—ch. 3

Delusion, Psychiatric—The psychiatric delusion also contains a particle of truth; the patient's conviction issues from this and extends to the whole delusional fabrication surrounding it.
M & M—Part III, Section II

DREAMS

Dreams, from above and from below—Dreams from below are those which are provoked by the strength of an unconscious (repressed) wish which has found a means of being represented in some of the day's residues. Dreams from above correspond to thoughts or intentions of the day before which have contrived during the night to obtain reinforcement from repressed material which is debarred from the ego.
TPDI

Dreams, Anxiety—Anxiety dreams do not contradict the wish-fulfilling function of the dream.
NILP—ch. 1

Anxiety in dreams is an anxiety-problem and not a dream-problem.
IoD—ch. 7

The anxiety in dreams may of course be of a psychoneurotic character, originating in psycho-sexual excitation, in which case, the anxiety corresponds to repressed libido. Then this anxiety, like the whole anxiety-dream, has the significance of a neurotic symptom, and we stand at the dividing-line where the wish-fulfilling tendency of dreams is frustrated. But in other anxiety-dreams the feeling of anxiety comes from somatic sources (as in the case of persons suffering from pulmonary or cardiac trouble, with occasional difficulty in breathing), and then it is used to help

such strongly suppressed wishes to attain fulfilment in a dream, the dreaming of which from psychic motives would have resulted in the same release of anxiety. It is not difficult to reconcile these two apparently contradictory cases. When two psychic formations, an affective inclination and a conceptual content, are intimately connected, either one being actually present will evoke the other, even in a dream; now the anxiety of somatic origin evokes the suppressed conceptual content, now it is the released conceptual content, accompanied by sexual excitement, which causes the release of anxiety. In the one case it may be said that a somatically determined affect is psychically interpreted; in the other case all is of psychic origin, but the content which has been suppressed is easily replaced by a somatic interpretation which fits the anxiety.
IoD—ch. 5

Dreams, Anxiety of Examination—We have had increasing confirmation of the fact that the anxiety-dream of examination occurs when the dreamer is anticipating a responsible task on the following day, with the possibility of disgrace.
IoD—ch. 5

Dreams, Counter-Wish—In the sexual constitution of many persons there is a masochistic component, which has arisen through the conversion of the aggressive, sadistic component into its opposite. Such people are called "ideal" masochists if they seek pleasure not in the bodily pain which may be inflicted upon them, but in humiliation and psychic chastisement. It is obvious that such persons may have counter-wish-dreams and disagreeable dreams, yet these are for them nothing more than wish-fulfilments, which satisfy their masochistic inclinations.
IoD—ch. 4

Dreams, Childhood Experiences in—If we turn from the manifest dream-content to the dream-thoughts which are revealed only on analysis, the experiences of childhood may be found to recur even in dreams whose content would not have led us to suspect anything of the sort. . . . *The child with all his impulses survives in the dream.* As a rule, of course, a scene from childhood is represented in the manifest dream-content only by an allusion, and must be disentangled from the dream by interpretation. The citation of examples of this kind cannot be very convincing, because any guarantee that they are really experiences of childhood is lacking; if they belong to an earlier period of life, they are no longer recognized by our memory. The conclusion that such childish experiences recur at all in dreams is justified in psychoanalytic work by a great number of factors, which in their combined results appear to be sufficiently reliable. But when, for the purposes of dream-interpretation such references to childish experiences are torn out of their context they may not perhaps seem very impressive.
IoD—ch. 5

Dreams, Children's—The dreams of little children are often simple fulfilments of wishes, and for this reason are, as compared with the dreams of adults, by no means interesting. They present no problem to be solved, but they are invaluable as affording proof that the dream, in its inmost essence, is the fulfilment of a wish. I have been able to collect several examples of such dreams from the material furnished by my own children.
IoD—ch. 3

Dreams, Classification of—We have kept our theory intact by dividing dreams into wish-dreams, anxiety-dreams, and punishment-dreams.
NILP—ch. 1

Dreams, Composite Formation in—The possibility of creating composite formations is one of the chief causes of the fantastic character so common in dreams, in that it introduces into the dream-content elements which could never have been objects of perception. The psychic process which occurs in the creation of composite formations is obviously the same as that which we employ in conceiving or figuring a dragon or a centaur in our waking senses. The only difference is that in the fantastic creations of waking life the impression intended is itself the decisive factor, while the composite formation in the dream is determined by a factor—the common feature in the dream-thoughts—which is independent of its form. Composite formations in dreams may be achieved in a great many different ways.
IoD—ch. 6

Similarity, agreement, community, are quite generally expressed in dreams by contraction into a *unity,* which is either already found in the dream-material or is newly created. The first case may be referred to as *identification,* the second as *composition.* Identification is used where the dream is concerned with persons, composition where things constitute the material to be unified; but compositions are also made of persons. Localities are often treated as persons.
IoD—ch. 6

Dreams as Compromise Structures—It must not be forgotten that dreams are invariably the product of a conflict, that they are a kind of compromise structure. Something that is a satisfaction for the unconscious id may for that very reason be a cause of anxiety for the ego.
OoPA

Dreams, Context of—All the dreams of one night belong to the same context; but it is by no means immaterial whether these dreams appear to the dreamer as a continuum, or whether they are organized in several pieces, and if so in how many. The number of pieces often corresponds to the same number of distinct nodal points in the chain of thoughts, which make up the latent dream-thoughts; or it may correspond to forces in the mental life of the dreamer which are struggling with one another, and each of which finds its main (though not its exclusive) expression in one particular part of the dream. A short introductory dream and a long main dream often stand to each other in the relation of condition and consequent; of this you will find a very clear example in the old lectures. A dream which the dreamer describes as 'somehow interpolated' really corresponds to a dependent clause in the dream-thoughts. NILP—ch. 1

Dreams, Critical Faculty in—Everything in dreams which occurs as the apparent functioning of the critical faculty is to be regarded, not as the intellectual performance of the dream-work, but as belonging to the substance of the dream-thoughts, and it has found its way from these, as a completed structure, into the manifest dream-content. IoD—ch. 6

Dreams, Exhibition—The nucleus of an exhibition-dream is furnished by one's own person which is seen not as that of a child, but as it exists in the present, and by the idea of scanty clothing which emerges indistinctly, owing to the superimposition of so many later situations of being partially clothed, or out of consideration for the censorship; to these elements are added the persons in whose presence one is ashamed. Strangely enough, those persons who are the objects of our sexual interest in childhood are omitted from all reproductions in dreams, in hysteria or in obsessional neu-rosis; paranoia alone restores the spectators, and is fanati-cally convinced of their presence, although they remain unseen. Furthermore, repression finds a place in the exhibition-dream. For the disagreeable sensation of the dream is, of course, the reaction on the part of the second psychic instance to the fact that the exhibitionistic scene which has been condemned by the censorship has never-theless succeeded in presenting itself. The only way to avoid this sensation would be to refrain from reviving the scene.

IoD—ch. 5

Dreams, Effect of External Stimuli on—The stimuli which occur during sleep are elaborated into a wish-fulfilment, of which the other components are the psychic remnants of daily experience with which we are already familiar. This combination, however, is not inevitable; we have seen that more than one kind of behaviour toward the physical stim-uli received during sleep is possible. Where this combina-tion is effected, a conceptual material for the dream-content has been found which will represent both kinds of dream-sources, the somatic as well as the psychic.

The nature of the dream is not altered when somatic ma-terial is added to the psychic dream-sources; it still remains a wish-fulfilment, no matter how its expression is deter-mined by the actual material available.

I should like to find room here for a number of peculiari-ties which are able to modify the significance of external stimuli for the dream. I imagine that a co-operation of indi-vidual, physiological and accidental factors, which depend on the circumstances of the moment, determines how one will behave in individual cases of more intensive objective

stimulation during sleep; habitual or accidental profundity of sleep, in conjunction with the intensity of the stimulus, will in one case make it possible so to suppress the stimulus that it will not disturb the sleeper, while in another case it will force the sleeper to wake, or will assist the attempt to subdue the stimulus by weaving it into the texture of the dream. In accordance with the multiplicity of these constellations, external objective stimuli will be expressed more rarely or more frequently in the case of one person than in that of another.
IoD—ch. 5

Dreams of Falling—Dreams of *falling* are more frequently characterized by anxiety. Their interpretation, when they occur in women, offers no difficulty, because they nearly always accept the symbolic meaning of falling, which is a circumlocution for giving way to an erotic temptation. We have not yet exhausted the infantile sources of the dream of falling; nearly all children have fallen occasionally, and then been picked up and fondled; if they fell out of bed at night, they were picked up by the nurse and taken into her bed.
IoD—ch. 6

I have good reasons for rejecting the explanation that it is the state of our dermal sensations during sleep, the sensation of the movements of the lungs, etc., that evokes dreams of flying and falling. I see that these very sensations have been reproduced from the memory to which the dream refers—and that they are, therefore, dream-content and not dream-sources.
IoD—ch. 5

Dreams of Fire—The interpretation of dreams of *fire* justifies a prohibition of the nursery, which forbids children to "play with fire" so that they may not wet the bed at night. These dreams also are based on reminiscences of the *enuresis nocturna* of childhood. In my *Fragment of an Analysis of Hysteria* I have given the complete analysis and synthesis of such a dream of fire in connection with the infantile history of the dreamer, and have shown for the representation of what maturer impulses this infantile material has been utilized.

IoD—ch. 6

Dreams of Flying—Why do so many people dream of flying? Psychoanalysis answers this question by stating that to fly or to be a bird in the dream is nothing but a concealment of another wish to the recognition of which we are led by more than one linguistic or real bridge. When the inquisitive child is told that a big bird like the stork brings the little children, when the ancients have formed the phallus winged . . . all these facts are only small fragments from a large collection which teaches us that the wish to be able to fly signifies in the dream nothing but the longing for the ability of sexual accomplishment. This is an early infantile wish. When the grown-up recalls his childhood, it appears to him as a joyful time, in which one is happy for the moment and looks to the future without any wishes; it is for this reason that he envies children. But the children themselves, if they could inform us about it, would probably give us different reports. It seems that childhood is not that blissful idyl into which we later distort it, that on the contrary children are lashed through the years of childhood by the wish to become big, and to imitate the grown-ups. This wish instigates all their playing. If in the course of their sexual investigation children feel that the grown-up knows something wonderful concerning the mysterious and yet so

important realm that they are prohibited from knowing or doing, they are seized with a violent wish to know it, and dream of it in the form of flying, or prepare this disguise of the wish for their later flying dreams. Thus aviation, which has attained its aim in our times, has also its infantile erotic roots.
LDV—ch. 6

Dream, Function of—Under certain conditions the dream can only achieve its end in a very incomplete way, or has to abandon it entirely; an unconscious fixation to the trauma seems to head the list of these obstacles to the dream-function. The sleeper has to dream, because the nightly relaxation of repression allows the upward thrust of the traumatic fixation to become active; but sometimes his dream-work, which endeavours to change the memory traces of the traumatic event into a wish-fulfilment, fails to operate. In these circumstances the result is that one becomes sleepless; one gives up all idea of sleep because of one's fear of the failure of the dream-function. The traumatic neurosis is an extreme case, but one must also attribute a traumatic character to infantile experiences as well; so one need not be surprised if lesser disturbances of the function of the dream occur in other circumstances.
NILP—ch. 1

Dreams, Inversion in—The dream-work is able to dispose of the affects of the dream-thoughts in yet another way than by admitting them or reducing them to zero. *It can transform them into their opposites.*
IoD—ch. 6
    Inversion, or transformation into the opposite, is one of

the most favoured and most versatile methods of representation which the dream-work has at its disposal.

Besides the inversion of content, the temporal inversion must not be overlooked.
IoD—ch. 6

Dreams take the liberty of representing any element whatever by its desired opposite, so that it is at first impossible to tell, in respect of any element which is capable of having an opposite, whether it is contained in the dream-thoughts in the negative or the positive sense.
IoD—ch. 6

Dream, Manifest—We call what one usually refers to as the dream, the dream-text or the *manifest* dream.
NILP—ch. 1

Dreams, Material of—The dream may select its material from any period of life, provided only that a chain of thought leads back from the experiences of the day of the dream (the "recent" impressions) of that earlier period.
IoD—ch. 5

Dream as a Pathological Product—The dream is a pathological product, the first member of the series which includes the hysterical symptom, the obsession and the delusion among its members; it is differentiated from the others by its transitoriness and by the fact that it occurs under conditions which are part of normal life.
NILP—ch. 1

Dreams, Prophetic—The belief in prophetic dreams numbers many adherents, because it can be supported by the fact that some things really so happen in the future as they

were previously foretold by the wish of the dream. But in
this, there is little to be wondered at, as many far-reaching
deviations may be regularly demonstrated between a
dream and the fulfillment which the credulity of the
dreamer prefers to neglect.
PEL—ch. 10

There can, indeed, be no doubt that there are such things
as prophetic dreams, in the sense that their content gives
some sort of picture of the future; the only question is
whether these predictions coincide to any noticeable extent
with what really happens subsequently.
OSD

Dream as a Psychosis—A dream, then, is a psychosis, with
all the absurdities, delusions and illusions of a psychosis.
No doubt it is a psychosis which has only a short duration,
which is harmless and even performs a useful function,
which is brought about with the subject's consent and is
ended by an act of his will. Nevertheless it *is* a psychosis,
and we learn from it that even so deep-going a modification
of mental life as this can be undone and can give place to
normal functioning.
OoPA—ch. 6

Dreams, Punishment—Even punishment-dreams are
wish-fulfilments but they do not fulfil the wishes of the instinctual impulses, but those of the critical, censuring and
punishing function of the mind. If we are faced with a pure
punishment-dream, a simple mental operation will enable
us to reinstate the wish-dream to which the punishment-
dream was the proper rejoinder; on account of this repudia-
tion, the punishment-dream has appeared in place of the
wish-dream as the manifest one.
NILP—ch. 1

Dreams, Secondary Elaboration in—There is to be considered a more or less non-constant factor, the so-called secondary elaboration, that makes its appearance after the dream has come into consciousness as an object of perception. When the dream has come into consciousness, we treat it in exactly the same way that we treat any content of perception; we try to fill in the gaps, we add connecting links, and often enough we let ourselves in for serious misunderstandings.
NILP—ch. 1

Dream and Its Relationship to Sleep—Throughout the whole of our sleep we are just as certain that we are dreaming as we are certain that we are sleeping.
IoD—ch. 7

Every dream is an *attempt* to put aside a disturbance of sleep by means of a wish-fulfillment. The dream is thus the guardian of sleep. This attempt can be more or less completely successful; it can also fail—in which case the sleeper wakes up, apparently aroused by the dream itself.
OoPA—ch. 5

Dreams, Influence of Somatic Stimuli on—The general aggregate of bodily sensation must undoubtedly be included among the dominant dream-stimuli of internal bodily origin. Not that it is capable of supplying the dream-content; but it forces the dream-thoughts to make a choice from the material destined to serve the purpose of representation in the dream-content, inasmuch as it brings within easy reach that part of the material which is adapted to its own character, and holds the rest at a distance. Moreover, this general feeling, which survives from the preceding day, is of course connected with the psychic residues that are significant for the dream. Moreover, this feeling itself may be either main-

tained or overcome in the dream, so that it may, if it is painful, veer round into its opposite.
IoD—ch. 5

If the external nerve-stimuli and the inner bodily stimuli are sufficiently intense to compel psychic attention, they represent—that is, if they result in dreaming at all, and not in waking—a fixed point for dream-formation, a nucleus in the dream-material, for which an appropriate wish-fulfilment is sought, just as well as mediating ideas between two psychical dream-stimuli are sought. To this extent it is true of a number of dreams that the somatic element dictates the dream-content. In this extreme case even a wish that is not actually present may be aroused for the purpose of dream-formation. But the dream cannot do otherwise than represent a wish in some situation as fulfilled; it is, as it were, confronted with the task of discovering what wish can be represented as fulfilled by the given sensation. Even if this given material is of a painful or disagreeable character, yet it is not unserviceable for the purposes of dream-formation. The psychic life has at its disposal even wishes whose fulfilment evokes displeasure, which seems a contradiction, but becomes perfectly intelligible if we take into account the presence of two sorts of psychic instance and the censorship that subsists between them. If sensations of a disagreeable character which originate from somatic sources are present during sleep, this constellation is utilized by the dream-activity to procure the fulfilment—with more or less maintenance of the censorship—of an otherwise suppressed wish.
IoD—ch. 5

Dreams, Sources of—The source of a dream may be:—
(a) A recent and psychologically significant event which is directly represented in the dream.

(b) Several recent and significant events, which are combined by the dream into a single whole.

(c) One or more recent and significant events, which are represented in the dream-content by allusion to a contemporary but indifferent event.

(d) A subjectively significant experience (recollection, train of thought), which is *constantly* represented in the dream by allusion to a recent but indifferent impression. IoD—ch. 5

Dreams, Speech in—When a spoken utterance, expressly distinguished as such from a thought, occurs in a dream, it is an invariable rule that the dream-speech has originated from a remembered speech in the dream-material. The wording of the speech has either been preserved in its entirety or has been slightly altered in expression; frequently the dream-speech is pieced together from different recollections of spoken remarks; the wording has remained the same, but the sense has perhaps become ambiguous, or differs from the wording. Not infrequently the dream-speech serves merely as an allusion to an incident in connection with which the remembered speech was made. IoD—ch. 6

Dreams of Swimming—People who dream often, and with great enjoyment, of *swimming*, cleaving the waves, etc., have usually been bed-wetters and they now repeat in the dream a pleasure which they have long since learned to forego. IoD—ch. 6

Dreams, Theory of—This theory occupies a peculiar position in the history of psycho-analysis; it marks a turning-point. With the theory of dreams, analysis passed from

being a psychotherapeutic method to being a psychology of the depths of human nature.
NILP—ch. 1

Dreams, Unification Compulsion in—If the day has brought us two or more experiences which are worthy to evoke a dream, the dream will blend the allusion of both into a single whole: it obeys *a compulsion to make them into a single whole.* I am persuaded to advance the proposition that a dream works under a kind of compulsion which forces it to combine into a unified whole all the sources of dream-stimulation which are offered to it.
IoD—ch. 5

Dream and Wish-Fulfillment—I believe that the *conscious wish becomes effective in exciting a dream only when it succeeds in arousing a similar unconscious wish which reinforces it.*
IoD—ch. 7
 The dream is the (disguised) fulfilment of a (suppressed, repressed) wish.
IoD—ch. 4
 In every dream an instinctual wish is displayed as fulfilled.
NILP—ch. 1
 Children's dreams leave us in no doubt that a wish unfulfilled during the day may instigate a dream.
IoD—ch. 7
 Perhaps this collection will suffice to prove that frequently, and under the most complex conditions, dreams may be noted which can be understood only as wish-fulfilments, and which present their content without concealment. In most cases these are short and simple dreams, and they stand in pleasant contrast to the confused and overloaded dream-compositions which have almost exclusively at-

tracted the attention of the writers on the subject. But it will repay us if we give some time to the examination of these simple dreams. The simplest dreams of all are, I suppose, to be expected in the case of children whose psychic activities are certainly less complicated than those of adults.
IoD—ch. 3

DREAM-CENSOR—The conflict of two psychic factors, which we—roughly—call the repressed unconscious and the conscious, dominates our lives, and the resistance against the interpretation of dreams, the hall-mark of the dream-censorship, is none other than the repression-resistance which keeps these two factors apart.
NILP—ch. 1

The fact of dream-censorship shows that enough repressive resistance remains operative even during sleep.
NILP—ch 1

The resistance which we come across during the process of dream-interpretation must play some part in the formation of the dream as well. . . . Resistance is the sure sign of a conflict. There must be a force present which is trying to express something, and another which is striving to prevent its expression. What comes into being as the manifest dream may, therefore, be regarded as comprising all the solutions to which the battle between these two opposing forces can be reduced. At one point one of the forces may have been able to get through what it wanted to say, at another the counteracting force may have succeeded in abolishing the intended communication entirely, or may have substituted for it something which betrays no sign of it. The most usual cases, and those which are the most characteristic of the process of dream-formation, are those in which the conflict results in a compromise, so that the communicating force can indeed say what it wants to say, but not in the way

it wants to say it; it is toned down, distorted and made un-recognizable. If therefore the dream does not faithfully rep-resent the dream-thoughts, if a process of interpretation is necessary to bridge the gulf between the two, this is the re-sult of the counteracting, inhibiting and restraining force whose existence we have inferred from perceiving the resis-tance in dream-interpretation. So long as we regarded the dream as an isolated phenomenon, independent of other psychological formations which are allied to it, we called this force the *dream-censor*.
NILP—ch. 1

DREAM-CONDENSATION—The laws governing uncon-scious processes, which come to light in this manner, are re-markable enough and suffice to explain the greater part of what seems strange to us about dreams. Above all there is a striking tendency to *condensation*, an inclination to form fresh unities out of elements which in our waking thoughts we should certainly have kept separate. As a consequence of this, a single element of the manifest dream often stands for a whole number of latent dream-thoughts, as though it were a combined allusion to all of them; and in general the dimen-sions of a manifest dream are extraordinarily small in com-parison with the wealth of material from which it has sprung.
OoPA—ch. 5

On other occasions and even much more frequently, the condensation work of the dream produces no composi-tions, but pictures which closely resemble an object or per-son up to a certain addition or variation which comes from another source.
WRU—ch. II

DREAM-CONTENT—The peculiar mode of operation, whose most striking function we recognize in the dream content, should not be attributed only to the sleeping state of the psychic life, when we possess abundant proof of its activity during the waking state in faulty actions. The same connection also forbids us from assuming that these psychic processes which impress us as abnormal and strange, are determined by deep-seated decay of psychic activity or by morbid state of function.

PEL—ch. 10

For us a new psychic material interposes itself between the dream-content and the results of our investigations: the *latent* dream-content, or dream-thoughts, which are obtained only by our method. We develop the solution of the dream from this latent content, and not from the manifest dream-content. The dream-content appears to us as a translation of the dream-thoughts into another mode of expression, whose symbols and laws of composition we must learn by comparing the origin with the translation.

IoD—ch. 6

DREAM-DAY—In every dream we may find some reference to the experience of the *preceding day.*

IoD—ch. 5

DREAM-DISPLACEMENT—It becomes very probable that a psychic force expresses itself in the dream-work which, on the one hand, strips the elements of the high psychic value of their intensity and, on the other hand, *by means of overdetermination,* creates new significant values from elements of slight value, which new values then make their way into the dream-content. Now if this is the method of procedure, there has occurred in the process of dream-formation a *transference and displacement of the psychic intensities* of the individual elements, from which results the textual difference between the dream-content and the thought-content. The process which we here assume to be operative is actually the most essential part of the dream-work; it may fitly be called *dream-displacement*. *Dream-displacement and dream-condensation* are the two craftsmen to whom we may chiefly ascribe the structure of the dream.

I think it will be easy to recognize the psychic force which expresses itself in dream-displacement. The result of this displacement is that the dream-content no longer has any likeness to the nucleus of the dream-thoughts, and the dream reproduces only a distorted form of the dream-wish in the unconscious. But we are already acquainted with dream-distortion; we have traced it back to the censorship which one psychic instance in the psychic life exercises over another. Dream-displacement is one of the chief means of achieving this distortion. *Is fecit, cui profuit.* We must assume that dream-displacement is brought about by the influence of this censorship, the endopsychic defence.
IoD—ch. 6

Displacement usually occurs in such a way that a colourless and abstract expression of the dream-thought is exchanged for one that is pictorial and concrete.
IoD—ch. 6

DREAM-DISTORTION—The dream-content takes up remnants of trivial experiences as a manifestation of *dream-distortion* (by displacement), and we have recognized this dream-distortion as the work of a censorship operating between the two psychic instances.
IoD—ch. 5

The study of dream-work affords us an excellent example of the way in which unconscious material from the id—originally unconscious and repressed unconscious alike—forces itself upon the ego, becomes preconscious and, owing

to the efforts of the ego, undergoes the modifications which we call *dream-distortion*. There are no features of the dream which cannot be explained in this fashion.
OoPA—ch. 5

I regard the attribution of dream-distortion to the censorship as the central point of my conception of the dream.
IoD—ch. 6

There are, of course, dreams which are undisguised wish-fulfilments. Wherever a wish-fulfilment is unrecognizable and disguised there must be present a tendency to defend oneself against this wish, and in consequence of this defence the wish is unable to express itself save in a distorted form.

The detailed correspondence between the phenomena of censorship and the phenomena of dream-distortion justifies us in presupposing similar conditions for both. We should then assume that in every human being there exist, as the primary cause of dream-formation, two psychic forces (tendencies or systems), one of which forms the wish expressed by the dream, while the other exercises a censorship over this dream-wish, thereby enforcing on it a distortion.
IoD—ch. 4

Dream-Distortion as Prevention of Anxiety—An anxiety-dream occurs only when the censorship is entirely or partially overpowered, and on the other hand, the overpowering of the censorship is facilitated when the actual sensation of anxiety is already present from somatic sources. It thus becomes obvious for what purpose the censorship performs its office and practises dream-distortion; it does so *in order to prevent the development of anxiety or other forms of painful affect.*
IoD—ch. 5

DREAM-FORMATION—The unconscious impulse is the real creator of the dream, it provides the psychic energy required for its formation.
NILP—ch. 1

Roughly speaking, one can distinguish three general stages in the formation of the dream; first, the transference of the conscious day remnants into the unconscious, a transference in which the conditions of the sleeping state must co-operate; secondly, the actual dream-work in the unconscious; and thirdly, the regression of the elaborated dream material to the region of perception, whereby the dream becomes conscious.

The forces participating in the dream-formation may be recognized as the following: the wish to sleep; the sum of cathexis which still clings to the day remnants after the depression brought about by the state of sleep; the psychic energy of the unconscious wish forming the dream; and the opposing force of the *"censorship,"* which exercises its authority in our waking state, and is not entirely abolished during sleep. The task of dream-formation is, above all, to overcome the inhibition of the censorship, and it is just this task that is fulfilled by the displacement of the psychic energy within the material of the dream-thoughts.
WRU—ch. VI

Let me repeat the stages of dream-formation. The introduction: the wish to sleep, the voluntary withdrawal from the outside world. Two things follow from this: firstly, the possibility for older and more primitive modes of activity to manifest themselves, *i.e.* regression; and secondly, the decrease of the repression-resistance which weighs on the unconscious. As a result of this latter feature an opportunity for dream-formation presents itself, which is seized upon by the factors which are the occasion of the dream; that is to say, the internal and external stimuli which are in activity.

The dream which thus eventuates is already a compromise-formation; it has a double function: it is on the one hand in conformity with the ego ('egosyntonic'), since it subserves the wish to sleep by draining off the stimuli which would otherwise disturb it, while on the other hand it allows to a repressed impulse the satisfaction which is possible in these circumstances in the form of an hallucinatory wish-fulfilment. The whole process of dream-formation, which is permitted by the sleeping ego, is, however, under the control of the censorship, a control which is exercised by what is left of the forces of repression. I cannot explain the process more simply; it is not in itself simpler than that.
NILP—ch. 1

Dream Formation, Share of the Id in—The evidence of the share taken by the unconscious id in the formation of dreams is abundant and convincing. *(a)* Memory is far more comprehensive in dreams than in waking life. Dreams bring up recollections which the dreamer has forgotten, which are inaccessible to him when he is awake. *(b)* Dreams make an unlimited use of linguistic symbols, the meaning of which is for the most part unknown to the dreamer. Our experience, however, enables us to establish their sense. They probably originate from earlier phases in the development of speech. *(c)* Memory very often reproduces in dreams impressions from the dreamer's early childhood of which we can definitely assert not only that they had been forgotten but that they had become unconscious owing to repression. This is the explanation of the help—usually indispensable—afforded to us by dreams when, in the course of the analytic treatment of the neuroses, we attempt to reconstruct the early life of the dreamer. *(d)* Beyond this, dreams bring to light material which could not originate either from the dreamer's adult life or from his forgotten

childhood. We are obliged to regard it as part of the *archaic heritage* which a child brings with him into the world, before any experience of his own, as a result of the experiences of his ancestors.
OoPA—ch. 5

Dream-Formation, the Role of Sleep in—The state of sleep makes dream-formation possible by reducing the endopsychic censorship.
IoD—ch. 7

DREAM-INTERPRETATION—There is a psychological technique which makes it possible to interpret dreams, and on the application of this technique, every dream will reveal itself as a psychological structure, full of significance, and one which may be assigned to a specific place in the psychic activities of the waking state.
IoD—ch. 1

The dream often appears to have several meanings; not only may several wish-fulfilments be combined in it, as our examples show, but one meaning or one wish-fulfilment may conceal another, until in the lowest stratum one comes upon the fulfilment of a wish from the earliest period of childhood; and here again it may be questioned whether the word "often" at the beginning of this sentence may not more correctly be replaced by "constantly."
IoD—ch. 5

We have got to turn the manifest dream into the latent dream, and we have to show how the latter became the former in the mental life of the dreamer. The first bit is a practical problem, it comes under the heading of *dream-interpretation,* and requires a technique; the second is a theoretical problem, its solution should be the explanation of the hypothetical *dream-work,* and can only be a theory.
NILP—ch. 1

It is impossible to interpret a dream unless one knows the relevant associations of the dreamer.
NILP—ch. 1

Dream-Interpretation, Resistance in—The work of interpretation is carried on in the face of resistance, which may vary from an imperceptible amount to an amount so great that we cannot overcome it—at any rate with the means which are at present at our disposal. We are right in supposing that the longer and the more circuitous the chain of associations, the stronger is the resistance. And in the forgetting of dreams, too, we sense the same influence.
NILP—ch. 1

Dreams, Semantics in—We cannot dismiss the conjecture, which forces itself on us psychiatrists, that we should understand the language of dreams better and translate it more easily if we knew more about the development of language.
ASPW

Dream-Interpretation, Technique of—We ask the dreamer as well to free himself from the impression of the manifest dream, to switch his attention from the dream as a whole to individual parts of its content, and to tell us one after another the things that occur to him in connection with these parts, what associations come into his mind when he turns his mental eye on to each of them separately. In what order shall we get the patient to take the parts of his dream? Here we have a variety of courses open to us. We can simply follow the chronological order in which the dream has been presented to us in description. That is what one might call the strictest, the classical method. Or we can ask the dreamer to look for the *residue of the previous day* in his dream, because experience has taught us that in almost every dream is incorporated a memory trace of, or an allusion to, an event (or it may be several events) of the previous day [the "dream day"]; and if we follow up these links we often discover all of a sudden the bridge from the apparently remote dream-world to the real life of the patient. Or else we tell him to begin with those elements in the dream-content which have struck him on account of their clarity and sensuous force. We happen to know that it is particularly easy for him to obtain associations to such elements. It makes no difference by which of these ways we choose to reach the associations we are looking for. But let us have no misunderstanding. The associations to the dream are not the latent dream-thoughts. These are contained, but not completely contained, in the associations. NILP—ch. 1

DREAM-THOUGHTS—The *content* of the dream-thoughts is reproduced by the apparent thinking in our dreams, but not *the relations of the dream-thoughts to one another*, in the determination of which relations thinking consists.
IoD—ch. 6

Dream-Thoughts, Latent—We call what we are looking for, what we, as it were, suspect to lie behind the dream, the *latent* dream-thoughts.
NILP—ch. 1

Their dominating element is the repressed impulse, which has obtained some kind of expression, toned down and disguised though it may be, by associating itself with stimuli which happen to be there and by tucking itself in the residue of the day before.
NILP—ch 1

DREAM-WORK—We have our distinction between *manifest* dream-material and *latent* dream-thoughts. The process which produces the former out of the latter is described as *dream-work*.
OoPA—ch. 5

The function of the dream-work may be described in the following manner: A structure of thoughts, mostly very complicated, which has been built up during the day and not brought to settlement—a day remnant—clings firmly even during night to the energy which it had assumed—the underlying center of interest—and thus threatens to disturb sleep. This day remnant is transformed into a dream by the dream-work and in this way rendered harmless to sleep. But in order to make possible its employment by the dream-work, this day remnant must be capable of being cast into the form of a wish, a condition that is not difficult to fulfill. The wish emanating from the dream-thoughts forms the first step and later on the nucleus of the dream. Experience gained from analyses—not the theory of the dream—teaches us that with children a fond wish left from the waking state suffices to evoke a dream, which is coherent and senseful, but almost always short, and easily recognizable as a "wish fulfillment."
WRU—ch. VI

The psychic activity in dream-formation resolves itself into two achievements: the production of the dream-thoughts and the transformation of these into the dream-content. The dream-thoughts are perfectly accurate, and are formed with all the psychic profusion of which we are capable; they belong to the thoughts which have not become conscious, from which our conscious thoughts also result by means of a certain transposition. There is doubtless much in them that is worth knowing, and also mysterious, but these problems have no particular relation to our dreams, and cannot claim to be treated under the head of dream-problems. On the other hand we have the process which changes the unconscious thoughts into the dream-content, which is peculiar to the dream-life and characteristic of it. Now, this peculiar dream-work is much farther removed from the pattern of waking thought than has been supposed by even the most decided depreciators of the psychic activity in dream-formation. It is not so much that it is more negligent, more incorrect, more forgetful, more incomplete than waking thought; it is something altogether different, qualitatively, from waking thought, and cannot therefore be compared with it. It does not think, calculate, or judge at all, but limits itself to the work of transformation. It may be exhaustively described if we do not lose sight of the conditions which its product must satisfy. This product, the dream, has above all to be withdrawn from the censorship, and to this end the dream-work makes use of the *displacement of psychic intensities,* even to the transvaluation of all psychic values; thoughts must be exclusively or predominantly reproduced in the material of visual and acoustic memory-traces, and from this requirement there proceeds the *regard of the dream-work for representability,* which it satisfies by fresh displacements. Greater intensities have (probably) to be produced than are at the disposal of the night dream-thoughts, and this purpose is served by the extensive *condensation* to which the constituents of the dream-thoughts are subjected. Little attention is paid to the logical relations of the thought-material; they ultimately find a veiled representation in the *formal* peculiarities of the dream. The effects of the dream-thoughts undergo slighter alterations than their conceptual content. As a rule, they are suppressed; where they are preserved, they are freed from the concepts and combined in accordance with their simi-

larity. Only one part of the dream-work—the revision, variable in amount, which is effected by the partially awakened conscious thought—is at all consistent with the conception which the writers on the subject have endeavoured to extend to the whole performance of dream-formation.
IoD—ch. 6

Dream-Work and the Ego—With the help of the unconscious, every dream in the process of formation makes a demand upon the ego for the satisfaction of an instinct (if it originates from the id) or for the solution of a conflict, the removal of a doubt, or the making of a decision (if it originates from a residue of preconscious activity in waking life). The sleeping ego, however, is focused upon the wish to maintain sleep; it regards this demand as a disturbance and seeks to get rid of the disturbance. The ego achieves this by what appears to be an act of compliance: it meets the demand with what is in the circumstances the innocent fulfillment of a wish and thus disposes of the demand. This replacement of a demand by the fulfillment of a wish remains the essential function of dream-work.
OoPA—ch. 5

E

EATING—The most frequent disturbance of the nutritive function is anorexia through withdrawal of libido. Increased desire to eat is also not infrequent; there is also a compulsion to eat, motivated by a fear of starvation, which has been little studied. As an hysterical defense against eating, the symptom of vomiting is familiar. Refusal to eat as a reaction to anxiety belongs among the psychotic patterns of behavior (delusions of poisoning) .
PoA—ch. 1

EDUCATION—*Education* can without further hesitation be described as an incitement to the conquest of the pleasure-principle, and to its replacement by the reality-principle.
FMPF

EGO—We recognize in man a psychical organization which is interpolated between his sensory stimuli and perception of his bodily needs on the one hand, and his motor activity on the other: and which mediates between them with a certain purpose. We call this organization his "I."
[Ego]
QLA—ch. 2

The ego is the organized part of the id.
PoA—ch. 3

The ego is an organization; it is dependent on the free intercommunication of, and the possibility of reciprocal interplay between, all its constituent elements; its desexualized energy still gives evidence of its origin in its striving for union and unification, and this compulsion to synthesis increases in direct proportion to the strength which the ego attains.
PoA—ch. 3

The principal characteristics of the ego are these. In consequence of the relation which was already established between sensory perception and muscular action, the ego is in control of voluntary movement. It has the task of self-preservation. As regards *external* events, it performs that task by becoming aware of the stimuli from without, by storing up experiences of them (in the memory), by avoiding excessive stimuli (through flight), by dealing with moderate stimuli (through adaptation) and, finally, by learning to bring about appropriate modifications in the external world to its own advantage (through activity). As regards *internal* events, in relation to the id, it performs that task by gaining control over the demands of the instincts, by deciding whether they shall be allowed to obtain satisfaction, by postponing that satisfaction to times and circumstances favorable in the external world or by suppressing their excitations completely. Its activities are governed by considerations of the tensions produced by stimuli present within it or introduced into it. The raising of these tensions is in general felt as *unpleasure* and their lowering as *pleasure*. It is probable, however, that what is felt as pleasure or unpleasure is not the *absolute* degree of the tensions, but something in the rhythm of their changes. The ego pursues pleasure and seeks to avoid unpleasure. An increase in unpleasure which is expected and foreseen is met by a *signal of anxiety;* the occasion of this increase, whether it threatens from without or within, is called a danger. From time to time the ego gives up its connection with the external world and withdraws into the state of sleep, in which its organization undergoes far-reaching changes. It may be inferred from the state of sleep that that organization consists in a particular distribution of mental energy.

OoPA—ch. 1

. . . The ego owes its origin as well as the most important of its acquired characteristics to its relation to the real external world; and we are thus prepared to assume that the pathological states of the ego—in which it most approximates once again the id—are founded upon a cessation or slackening of that relation to the external world.

OoPA—ch. 8

The ego is principally determined by the individual's own experience, that is to say by accidental and current events.

OoPA—ch. 1

The severest demand upon the ego is probably the keeping down of the instinctual claims of the id, and for this end the ego is obliged to maintain great expenditures of energy upon anti-cathexes. But the claims made by the super-ego, too, may become so powerful and so remorseless that the ego may be crippled, as it were, for its other tasks.

OoPA—ch. 6

No such purpose as that of keeping itself alive or of protecting itself from dangers by means of anxiety can be attributed to the id. That is the business of the ego, which is also concerned with discovering the most favorable and least perilous method of obtaining satisfaction, taking the external world into account.

OoPA—ch. 2

The *ego* was developed out of the cortical layer of the id, which, being adapted for the reception and exclusion of stimuli, is in direct contact with the external world. Its psychological function consists in raising the processes in the id to a higher dynamic level (perhaps by transforming freely mobile into bound energy, such as corresponds to the preconscious condition); its constructive function consists in interposing, between the demand made by an instinct and the action that satisfies it, an intellective activity which, after considering the present state of things and weighing up earlier experiences, endeavors by means of experimental actions to calculate the consequences of the proposed line of conduct.

OoPA—ch. 8

Ego, Split in the—The ego can take itself as object, it can treat itself like any other object, observe itself, criticize itself, and do Heaven knows what besides with itself. In such a case one part of the ego stands over against the other. The ego can, then, be split; it splits when it performs many of its functions, at least for the time being. The parts can afterwards join up again.

NILP—ch. 3

The view which postulates that in all psychoses there is a *split in the ego* could not demand so much notice, if it were not for the fact that it turns out to apply also to other conditions more like the neuroses and, finally, to the neuroses themselves.

OoPA—ch. 8

EGO-LIBIDO—We have laid down the concept of libido as a force of variable quantity by which processes and transformations in the spheres of sexual excitement can be measured. This libido we distinguished from the energy which is at the basis of the psychic processes in general as far as their special origin is concerned, and we thus attribute to it also a qualitative character. In separating libidinal from other psychic energy, we give expression to the assumption that the sexual processes of the organism are differentiated from the nutritional processes through a special chemism. The analyses of perversions and psychoneuroses have taught us that this sexual excitement is furnished not only from the so-called sexual parts alone, but from all organs of the body. We thus formulate for ourselves the concept of a *libido-quantum*, the psychic representative of which we designate as the *ego-libido*. The production, increase, distribution, and displacement of this ego-libido, thus offer the possible explanation for the manifest psychosexual phenomena.

But this ego-libido can only become conveniently accessible to psychoanalytic study if its psychic energy is invested or occupied (cathexis) in sexual objects; that is, if it becomes object-libido. We can then see it as it concentrates and fixes itself on objects, or as it leaves those objects and passes over to others, from which position it directs the individual's sexual activity; that is, as it leads to partial and temporary extinction of the libido. Psychoanalysis of the so-called transference neuroses (hysteria and compulsion neurosis) offers us here a reliable insight.

TCTS III

EGO-RESISTANCE—The resistance which we have to overcome in analysis is produced by the ego, which clings tenaciously to its anticathexes. The ego finds it difficult to turn its attention to perceptions and ideas the avoidance of which it had until then made a rule, or to acknowledge as belonging to it impulses which constitute the most complete antithesis to those familiar to it as its own. Our com-

bating of resistance in the analysis is based upon this conception of it. We make the resistance conscious where, as so often, in consequence of its connection with the repressed, it is unconscious; we oppose logical arguments to it when or after it has become conscious, promising the ego advantages and rewards if it renounces the resistance. As regards the resistance of the ego there is therefore nothing to call into question or to correct. On the other hand, the question is whether resistance alone covers the situation that confronts us in analysis. We experience the fact that the ego still finds it difficult to nullify its repressions even after it has resolved to give up its resistances, and we have designated the phase of strenuous effort which follows upon this laudable resolution as the period of "working through."
POA—ch 11

EROS—We have decided to assume the existence of only two basic instincts, *Eros* and the *destructive instinct*. (The contrast between the instincts of self-preservation and of the preservation of the species, as well as the contrast between ego-love and object-love, fall within the bounds of Eros.) The aim of the first of these basic instincts is to establish ever greater unities and to preserve them thus—in short, to bind together.
OoPA—ch. 2

ETHICS—Ethics must be regarded as a therapeutic effort: as an endeavour to achieve something through the standards imposed by the superego which had not been attained by the work of civilization in other ways.
C & D—ch. 8

We may say that a part of its [ethics] precepts is explained rationally by the necessity of marking off the rights of the community to the individual, those of the individual

to the community, and those of individuals to one another. What, however, appears mysterious, grandiose, and mystically self-evident owes its character to its connection with religion, its origin in the will of the father.
M & M—Part III, Section II

EXHIBITIONISM—In the history of the childhood of neurotics exposure before children of the opposite sex plays a prominent part; in paranoia the delusion of being observed while dressing and undressing may be directly traced to these experiences; and among those who have remained perverse there is a class in whom the childish impulse is accentuated into a symptom: the class of *exhibitionists.*
IoD—ch. 5

F

FETISH, FETISHISM—This abnormality, which can be counted as one of the perversions, is, as is well known, based upon the patient, who is almost always male, not recognizing the fact that women have no penis—a fact which is exceedingly distasteful to him because of the evidence it affords of the possibility of his being castrated himself. He therefore rejects the perception of his own senses, which showed him that women's genitals lack a penis, and holds fast to the opposite conviction. The rejected perception, however, does not remain entirely without effects, for, in spite of everything, the patient has not the courage to assert that he really saw a penis. He snatches hold of something else instead—a part of the body or some other object—and attributes to it the rôle of the penis which he cannot do without. It is usually something that he actually saw at the moment at which he saw the woman's genitals, or it is something which can suitably serve as a symbolic substitute for the penis. Now it would not be right to describe this process which accompanies the formation of a fetish as a split in the ego; it is a compromise formed with the aid of displacement, such as we have been familiar with in dreams.
OoPA—ch. 8

Fetish, Shoe and Foot as—The fetish-like reverence for the feminine foot and shoe seems to take the foot only as a substitutive symbol for the once revered and since then missed member of the woman.
LDV—ch. 3

FIRE—I conjecture that, in order to possess himself of fire, it was necessary for man to renounce the homosexually-tinged desire to extinguish it by a stream of urine.
APF

FIXATION—Fixation can be described in this way. One instinct or instinctual component fails to accompany the rest along the anticipated normal path of development, and, in consequence of this inhibition in its development, it is left behind at a more infantile stage. The libidinal current in question then behaves in regard to later psychological structures as though it belonged to the system of the unconscious, as though it were repressed. [See also *Parents; Trauma, Fixation to the.*]
ParDP—ch. 3

FORGETTING

Forgetting, Mechanism of—I can perhaps give the following outline concerning the mechanism of actual forgetting. The memory material succumbs in general to two influences, condensation and distortion. Distortion is the work of the tendencies dominating the psychic life and directs itself above all against the affective remnants of memory traces which maintain a more resistive attitude towards condensation. The traces which have grown indifferent, merge into a process of condensation without opposition; in addition, it may be observed that tendencies of distortion also feed on the indifferent material, because they have not been gratified where they wished to manifest themselves. As these processes of condensation and distortion continue for long periods, during which all fresh experiences act upon the transformation of the memory content, it is our belief that it is time that makes memory uncertain and indistinct. It is quite probable that in forgetting, there can really be no question of a direct function of time. From the repressed memory traces, it can be verified that they suffer no changes even in the longest periods. The unconscious, at all events, knows no time limit. The most important, as well as the most peculiar character of psychic fixation consists in the fact that all impressions are, on the one hand, retained in the same form as they were received, and also in the forms that they have assumed in their further development. This state of affairs cannot be elucidated by any comparison from any other sphere. By virtue of this theory, every former state of the memory content may thus be restored, even though all original relations have long been replaced by newer ones.

PEL—ch. 10

Forgetting of Names—I was led to examine exhaustively the phenomenon of temporary forgetfulness through the observation of certain peculiarities, which, although not general, can, nevertheless, be seen clearly in some cases. In these, there is not only *forgetfulness,* but also false *recollection;* he who strives for the escaped name brings to consciousness others—substitutive names—which, although immediately recognized as false, nevertheless obtrude themselves with great tenacity. The process which should lead to the reproduction of the lost name is, as it were, displaced, and thus brings one to an incorrect substitute.

Now it is my assumption that the displacement is not left

to psychic arbitrariness, but that it follows lawful and rational paths. In other words, I assume that the substitutive
name (or names) stands in direct relation to the lost name,
and I hope, if I succeed in demonstrating this connection, to
throw light on the origin of the forgetting of names. . . .
When we recapitulate the conditions for forgetting a name
with faulty recollection we find: (1) a certain disposition to
forget the name; (2) a process of suppression which has
taken place shortly before; and (3) the possibility of estab-
lishing an *outer* association between the concerned name
and the element previously suppressed. The last condition
will probably not have to be much overrated, for the slight-
est claim on the association is apt in most cases to bring it
about. But it is a different and farther-reaching question
whether such outer association can really furnish the
proper condition to enable the suppressed element to disturb the reproduction of the desired name, or whether after
all a more intimate connection between the two themes is
not necessarily required. On superficial consideration, one
may be willing to reject the latter requirement and consider
the temporal meeting in perfectly dissimilar contents as
sufficient. But on more thorough examination, one finds
more and more frequently that the two elements (the repressed and the new one) connected by an outer association, possess besides a connection in content. . . . I believe
that one is not justified in separating the cases of name-
forgetting with faulty recollection from those in which incorrect substitutive names have not obtruded themselves.
. . . Besides the simple forgetting of proper names, there is
another forgetting which is motivated by repression.
PEL—ch. 1

    The mechanism of forgetting, or rather of losing or tem-
porary forgetting of a name, consists in the disturbance of
the intended reproduction of the name through a strange

stream of thought unconscious at the time. Between the disturbed name and the disturbing complex, there exists a connection either from the beginning or such a connection has been formed—perhaps by artificial means—through superficial (outer) associations.

The self-reference complex (personal, family or professional) proves to be the most effective of the disturbing complexes. . . . To avoid the awakening of pain through memory is one of the objects among the motives of these disturbances.

In general, one may distinguish two principal cases of name-forgetting; when the name itself touches something unpleasant, or when it is brought into connection with other associations which are influenced by such effects. Thus, names can be disturbed on their own account or on account of their nearer or more remote associative relations in the reproduction.

A review of these general principles readily convinces us that the temporary forgetting of a name is observed as the most frequent faulty action of our mental functions.

However, we are far from having described all the peculiarities of this phenomenon. I also wish to call attention to the fact that name-forgetting is extremely contagious. In a conversation between two persons, the mere mention of having forgotten this or that name by one often suffices to induce the same memory slip in the other. But wherever the forgetting is induced, the sought-for name easily comes to the surface.

There is also a continuous forgetting of names in which whole chains of names are withdrawn from memory. If, in the course of endeavoring to discover an escaped name, one finds others with which the latter is intimately connected, it often happens that these new names also escape. The forgetting thus jumps from one name to another, as if to

demonstrate the existence of a hindrance not to be easily removed.
PEL—ch. 3

In the case of forgetting names, *we are aware* that the substitutive names are *incorrect*.
PEL—ch. 4

FORTUNE-TELLERS—During the psycho-analytic treatment of patients I have had the impression that the activities of professional fortune-tellers provide an admirable opportunity for making really satisfactory observations of thought-transference.
NILP—ch. 2

FRIGIDITY, SEXUAL—The sexual frigidity of women is a phenomenon which is insufficiently understood. Sometimes it is psychogenic, and, if so, it is accessible to influence; but in other cases one is led to assume that it is constitutionally conditioned or even partly caused by an anatomical factor.
NILP—ch. 5

G

GUILT

Guilt Feeling—We know of two sources for feelings of guilt: that arising from the dread of authority and the later one from the dread of the super-ego. The first one compels us to renounce instinctual gratification; the other presses over and above this towards punishment, since the persistence of forbidden wishes cannot be concealed from the super-ego.
C & D—ch. 7

H

HAPPINESS—What is called happiness in its narrowest sense comes from the satisfaction—most often instantaneous—of pent-up needs which have reached great intensity, and by its very nature can only be a transitory experience.
C & D—ch. 2

HATE—It is noteworthy that in the use of the word "hate" no such intimate relation to sexual pleasure and the sexual function appears [as in "love"]: on the contrary, the painful character of the relation seems to be the sole decisive feature.
I & V

HERMAPHRODITISM—Science shows cases in which the sexual characteristics appear blurred so that the sexual distinction is difficult, especially on an anatomical basis. The genitals of such persons unite the male and female characteristics (hermaphroditism). In rare cases both parts of the sexual apparatus are well developed (true hermaphroditism), but usually both are stunted.
TCTS I

In both sexes the degree of physical hermaphroditism is to a great extent independent of the psychical hermaphroditism.
PHW

HERO-WORSHIP—The great majority of people have a strong need for authority which they can admire, to which they can submit, and which dominates and sometimes even ill-treats them. We have learned from the psychology of the individual whence comes this need of the masses. It is the longing for the father that lives in each of us from his childhood days, for the same father whom the hero of legend boasts of having overcome.
M & M—Part III, Section II

HOMOSEXUALITY—Analysis shows that in every case a homosexual attachment to an object has at one time been present and in most cases has persisted in a latent condition.
OoPA—ch. 3

Homosexuals are persons who, owing to the erotogenic importance of their own genitals, cannot do without a similar feature in their sexual object. In the course of their development from auto-erotism to object-love, they have remained at a point of fixation between the two.

There is absolutely no justification for distinguishing a special homosexual instinct. What constitutes a homosexual is a peculiarity not in his instinctual life but in his object-choice.
AP5B—ch. 3

Homosexuals, Male—Homosexual men who have started in our times an energetic action against the legal restrictions of their sexual activity are fond of representing themselves

through theoretical spokesmen as evincing a sexual variation, which may be distinguished from the very beginning,
as an intermediate stage of sex or as "a third sex." In other
words, they maintain that they are men who are forced by
organic determinants originating in the germ to find that
pleasure in the man which they cannot feel in the woman.
As much as one would wish to subscribe to their demands
out of humane considerations, one must nevertheless exercise reserve regarding their theories which were formulated
without regard for the psychogenesis of homosexuality. . . .
In all our male homosexuals there was a very intensive
erotic attachment to a feminine person, as a rule to the
mother, which was manifest in the very first period of childhood and later entirely forgotten by the individual. This attachment was produced or favored by too much love from
the mother herself, but was also furthered by the retirement
or absence of the father during the childhood period. . . .
Following this primary stage, a transformation takes place
whose mechanisms we know but whose motive forces we
have not yet grasped. The love of the mother cannot continue to develop consciously so that it merges into repression. The boy represses the love for the mother by putting
himself in her place, by identifying himself with her, and by
taking his own person as a model through the similarity of
which he is guided in the selection of his love object. He
thus becomes homosexual; as a matter of fact, he returns to
the stage of autoerotism, for the boys whom the growing
adult now loves are only substitutive persons or revivals of
his own childish person, whom he loves in the same way as
his mother loved him. We say that he finds his love object
on the road to narcissism, for the Greek legend called a boy
Narcissus to whom nothing was more pleasing than his
own mirrored image, and who became transformed into a
beautiful flower of this name.

Deeper psychological discussions justify the assertion that the person who becomes homosexual in this manner remains fixed in his unconscious on the memory picture of his mother. By repressing the love for his mother he conserves the same in his unconscious and henceforth remains faithful to her. When as a lover he seems to pursue boys, he really thus runs away from women who could cause him to become disloyal to his mother.
LDV—ch. 3

HYPNOSIS—Hypnosis is a case rather different from that of analysis. It is the inducement of an abnormal mental state, and at the present day is only employed, by laymen, for purposes of entertainment.
QLA—ch. 6

I

ID—To the oldest of the mental provinces or agencies we give the name of *id*. It contains everything that is inherited, that is present at birth, that is fixed in the constitution—above all, therefore, the instincts, which originate in the somatic organization and which find their first mental expression in the id in forms unknown to us.
OoPA—ch. 1

You must not expect me to tell you much that is new about the id, except its name. It is the obscure inaccessible part of our personality; the little we know about it we have learnt from the study of dream-work and the formation of neurotic symptoms, and most of that is of a negative character, and can only be described as being all that the ego is not. We can come nearer to the id with images, and call it a chaos, a cauldron of seething excitement. We suppose that it is somewhere in direct contact with somatic processes, and takes over from them instinctual needs and gives them mental expression, but we cannot say in what substratum this contact is made. These instincts fill it with energy, but it has no organization and no unified will, only an impulsion to obtain satisfaction for the instinctual needs, in accordance with the pleasure-principle. The laws of logic—

above all, the law of contradiction—do not hold for processes in the id. Contradictory impulses exist side by side without neutralizing each other or drawing apart; at most they combine in compromise formations under the overpowering economic pressure towards discharging their energy. There is nothing in the id which can be compared to negation, and we are astonished to find in it an exception to the philosophers' assertion that space and time are necessary forms of our mental acts. In the id there is nothing corresponding to the idea of time, no recognition of the passage of time, and (a thing which is very remarkable and awaits adequate attention in philosophic thought) no alteration of mental processes by the passage of time. . . . Naturally, the id knows no values, no good and evil, no morality. . . . Instinctual cathexes seeking discharge,—that, in our view, is all that the id contains.
NILP—ch. 3

The power of the id expresses the true purpose of the individual organism's life. This consists in the satisfaction of its innate needs. No such purpose as that of keeping itself alive or of protecting itself from dangers by means of anxiety can be attributed to the id. That is the business of the ego. . . .
OoPA—ch. 2

In the Id there are no conflicts; contradictions and antitheses exist side by side, and often equalize matters between themselves by compromise formations.
QLA—ch. 2

. . . Everything which goes on in the Id is unconscious and remains so. . . .
QLA—ch. 2

The id cannot be afraid, as the ego can; it is not an organization, and cannot estimate situations of danger.
PoA—ch 8

The core of our being, then, is formed by the obscure *id*, which has no direct relations with the external world and is accessible even to our own knowledge only through the medium of another agency of the mind. . . . The id, which is cut off from the external world, has its own world of perception. . . .

The id obeys the inexorable pleasure principle.
OoPA—ch. 8

ILLNESS

Illness, Advantage Gained by—Illness may be used as a protection—to palliate incapacity at work or among competitors, or in family life as a means to force sacrifices and demonstrations of affection from others, or impose one's will upon them. All this is comparatively on the surface, and we put it all together under the heading "advantage gained by illness"; the only remarkable thing is that the patient—his Ego—knows nothing of the whole connection of such motives with his resulting behavior.
QLA—ch. 5

Illness as Self-Punishment—It is very important for mental health that the Super-Ego should develop normally—that is, that it should become sufficiently depersonalized. It is precisely this that does not happen in the case of a neurotic, because his Œdipus complex does not undergo the right transformation. His Super-Ego deals with his Ego like a strict father with a child, and his idea of morality displays itself in primitive ways by making the Ego to submit to punishment by the Super-Ego. Illness is employed as a means for this "self-punishment." The neurotic has to behave as though he were mastered by guilt, which the illness serves to punish, and so to relieve him.
QLA—ch. 5

IMPOTENCE, PSYCHIC—The sexual function is subject to a great multiplicity of disturbances, the majority of which have the character of simple inhibitions. These are grouped together as psychic impotence.
PoA—ch. 1

Here again—as very probably in all neurotic disorders—the root of the trouble lies in an arrest occurring during the course of development of the libido to that ultimate form which may be called normal.
CPL—DEL

INDIVIDUAL PSYCHOLOGY—In reality Individual Psychology has very little to do with analysis, but, for certain historical reasons, lives a sort of parasitic existence at its expense. . . . The name itself is unsuitable, and seems to be a product of embarrassment; we cannot assent to any interference with its correct application as meaning the opposite of Group Psychology; for the matter of that our own concern is, first and foremost, the psychology of the human individual.
NILP—ch. 6

INFERIORITY

"Inferiority Complex"—As a matter of fact the phrase "inferiority-complex" is hardly ever used in psycho-analysis. It does not refer to anything which we regard as simple, let alone elementary.
NILP—ch. 3

Inferiority, Sense of—To trace it back to the perception in oneself of some organic disability or other, as the school of so-called Individual Psychologists like to do, seems to us a short-sighted error. The sense of inferiority has a strong

erotic basis. The child feels itself inferior when it perceives that it is not loved, and so does the adult as well. The only organ that is really regarded as inferior is the stunted penis—the girl's clitoris. But the major part of the sense of inferiority springs from the relationship of the ego to its super-ego, and, like the sense of guilt, it is an expression of the tension between them. The sense of inferiority and the sense of guilt are exceedingly difficult to distinguish. Perhaps we should do better if we regarded the former as the erotic complement to the sense of moral inferiority.
NILP—ch. 3

INHIBITION—Inhibition is the expression of a *functional limitation of the ego*—a limitation which may have a large variety of causes.
PoA—ch. 1

One may say of inhibitions, in fine, that they represent a limitation and restriction of ego functions, either precautionary or resulting from an impoverishment of energy.
PoA—ch. 1

The more general inhibitions of the ego follow a simple mechanism. When the ego is occupied with a psychic task of special difficulty, as for example by mourning, a wholesale suppression of affect, or by the necessity for holding constantly mounting sexual fantasies in check, it becomes so impoverished with respect to the energy available to it that it is driven to restrict its expenditure in many places at the same time like a speculator who has tied up his money in his various enterprises.
PoA—ch. 1

INSTINCT—The forces which we assume to exist behind the tensions caused by the needs of the id are called *instincts*. They represent the somatic demands upon mental life. Though they are the ultimate cause of all activity, they are by nature conservative; the state, whatever it may be, which a living thing has reached, gives rise to a tendency to re-establish that state so soon as it has been abandoned. It is possible to distinguish an indeterminate number of instincts and in common practice this is in fact done. For us, however, the important question arises whether we may not be able to derive all of these various instincts from a few fundamental ones. We have found that instincts can change their aim (by displacement) and also that they can replace one another—the energy of one instinct passing over to another. This latter process is still insufficiently understood. After long doubts and vacillations we have decided to assume the existence of only two basic instincts.

OoPA—ch. 2

Instinct in general is regarded as a kind of elasticity of living things, an impulsion towards the restoration of a situation which once existed but was brought to an end by some external disturbance.

ABS—ch. 5

An instinct differs from a stimulus in that it arises from sources of stimulation within the body, operates as a constant force, and is such that the subject cannot escape from it by flight as he can from an external stimulus. An instinct may be described as having a source, an object and an aim. The source is a state of excitation within the body, and its aim is to remove that excitation; in the course of its path from its source to the attainment of its aim the instinct becomes operative mentally.

NILP—ch. 4

Observation shows us that an instinct may undergo the following vicissitudes: reversal into its opposite, turning round upon the subject, repression, sublimation.

I & V

By the *impetus* of an instinct we understand its motor element, the amount of force or the measure of the demand upon energy which it represents.

The *aim* of an instinct is in every instance satisfaction, which can only be obtained by abolishing the condition of stimulation in the source of the instinct.

The *object* of an instinct is that in or through which it can achieve its aim.

By the *source* of an instinct is meant that somatic process in an organ or part of the body from which there results a stimulus represented in mental life by an instinct.

I & V

INTOXICATION—The crudest of the methods of influencing the body, but also the most effective, is the chemical one: that of intoxication . . . The services rendered by intoxicating substances in the struggle for happiness and in warding off misery rank so highly as a benefit that both individuals and races have given them an established position within their libido-economy. It is not merely the immediate gain in pleasure which one owes to them, but also a measure of that independence of the outer world which is so sorely craved.

C & D—ch. 2

INVERSION, INVERT—There are men for whom the sexual object is not woman but man, and there are women for whom it is not man but woman. Such *persons* are designated as contrary sexuals, or better, inverts, and the situation of such a relationship is called inversion. The number of such individuals is considerable, although it is difficult to estimate them accurately. . . . *Conception of Inversion.* The first studies of the inversion gave rise to the assumption that it was a sign of innate nervous degeneration. This harmonized with the fact that physicians first observed it among nervous persons, or among those giving such an impression. There are two elements which should be considered independently in this characterization: the congenitality, and the degeneration.... *Explanation of Inversions.* The nature of inversion is explained neither by the assumption that it is congenital nor that it is acquired. In the first case, we need to be told what there is in it of the congenital, unless we are satisfied with the roughest explanation, namely, that a person brings along a congenital sexual instinct connected with a definite sexual object. In the second case it is a question whether the manifold accidental influences suffice to explain the acquisition, unless there is something in the individual to meet it half way. The negation of this last factor is inadmissible according to our former conclusions.... *The Sexual Aim of the Invert.* The important fact to bear in mind is that no uniformity of the sexual aim can be attributed to inversion. Intercourse *per anum* in men by no means goes with inversion; masturbation is just as frequently the exclusive aim; and the limitation of the sexual aim to mere effusion of feelings is here even more frequent than in heterosexual love. In women, too, the sexual aims of the inverts are manifold, among which contact with the mucous membrane of the mouth seems to be preferred.

TCTS I

J

JEALOUSY—Jealousy is one of those affective states, like grief, that may be described as normal. If anyone appears to be without it, the inference is justified that it has undergone severe repression and consequently plays all the greater part in his unconscious mental life. The instances of abnormally intense jealousy met with in analytic work reveal themselves as constructed of three layers. The three layers or stages of jealousy may be described as (1) *competitive* or normal, (2) *projected,* and (3) *delusional* jealousy.
NM-JPH

L

LAY ANALYST—Analytical training certainly intersects the circle of medical training, but it does not comprise it nor is it comprised within it.
QLA—ch. 7

The preparation for analytical practice is no simple and easy matter; the work is hard and the responsibility heavy. But, anyone who has undergone such a discipline, has been analyzed, has grasped the psychology of the unconscious as it is known today, has become versed in the scientific aspects of sexuality, and has learned the delicate technique of psychoanalysis, the art of interpretation, the way to combat resistances, and to manage the transference—*that person is no longer a layman in the field of psychoanalysis.*
QLA—ch. 5

So far as the patient is concerned, it does not matter whether the analyst is a doctor or not, so long as the danger of a mistake as to his case is secured against by the prescribed medical opinion before the analysis begins, and, if required, during its course. For him, it is incomparably more important that the analyst should possess such personal qualities as will command his confidence, and that he should have acquired the knowledge and insight, and the experience, which alone can fit him for his task.
QLA—ch. 7

Lay analysts, as they are found practicing today, are not chance-comers, recruited and trained without discrimination, but persons of academic standing.
QLA—ch. 7

LIBIDO—Libido is a term used in the theory of the instincts for describing the dynamic manifestation of sexuality.
LT

It is difficult to say anything of the behavior of the libido in the id and in the superego. Everything that we know about it relates to the ego, in which the whole available amount of libido is at first stored up. We call this state of things absolute, primary *narcissism*. It continues until the ego begins to cathect the presentations of objects with libido—to change narcissistic libido into *object libido*.
OoPA—ch. 2

Libido participates in every instinctual manifestation, but not everything in that manifestation is libido.
C & D—ch. 6

LIES, CHILDREN'S—It is comprehensible that children should tell lies when in doing so they mimic the lies of grown-up people. But a number of the lies of well-brought-up children have a peculiar significance, and should cause their instructors to reflect rather than to be angry. These lies proceed from the influence of an excessive love motive.
IML

LITERATURE—I am of opinion that all the aesthetic pleasure we gain from the works of imaginative writers is of the same type as the "fore-pleasure," and that the true enjoyment of literature proceeds from the release of tensions in our minds.
RPDD

LOOKING, DESIRE FOR—The desire for looking becomes a perversion (a) when it is exclusively limited to the genitals; (b) when it becomes connected with the overcoming of loathing (voyeurs and onlookers at the functions of excretion); and (c) when instead of preparing for the normal sexual aim, it suppresses it.
TCTS I

LOVE—Love in itself, in the form of longing and deprivation, lowers the self-regard; whereas to be loved, to have love returned, and to possess the beloved object, exalts it again.
Narc

Being in love is based upon the simultaneous presence of directly sexual tendencies and of sexual tendencies that are inhibited in their aims, so that the object draws a part of the narcissistic ego-libido to itself. It is a condition in which there is only room for the ego and the object.
GPAE—ch. 12

Not to love before one gains full knowledge of the thing loved presupposes a delay which is harmful. When one finally reaches cognition, he neither loves nor hates properly; one remains beyond love and hatred. One has investigated instead of having loved.
LDV—ch. 1

Love, Sexual—One of the forms in which love manifests itself, sexual love, gives us our most intense experience of an overwhelming pleasurable sensation and so furnishes a prototype for our strivings after happiness.
C & D—ch. 2

M

MASOCHISM—Masochism comes under our observation in three shapes: as a condition under which sexual excitation may be roused; as an expression of feminine nature; and as a norm of behaviour. According to this one may distinguish an *erotogenic*, a *feminine*, and a *moral* type of masochism. The first, the erotogenic masochism, the lust of pain, is also to be found at bottom in the other forms; the concept of it can be supported on biological and constitutional grounds; it remains incomprehensible unless one can bring oneself to make certain assumptions about matters that are wrapt in obscurity. The third, in certain respects the most important form in which masochism appears, has only lately, as a sense of guilt that is for the most part unconscious, been properly appreciated by psycho-analysis; it already admits, however, of full explanation and of co-ordination into our previous knowledge. Feminine masochism, on the other hand, is the form most accessible to observation, least mysterious, and is comprehensible in all its relations.
EPM

MASTURBATION—An overwhelming aetiological importance is attributed by neurotics to their masturbatory practices. They make them responsible for all their troubles, and we have the greatest difficulty in getting them to believe that they are wrong. But as a matter of fact we ought to admit that they are in the right, for masturbation is the executive agent of infantile sexuality, from the faulty development of which they are suffering. The difference is that what the neurotics are blaming is the masturbation of the pubertal stage; the infantile masturbation, which is the one that really matters, has for the most part been forgotten by them.

NILP—ch. 5

MELANCHOLIA—Melancholia, or more accurately the melancholic attack. In this disease, about whose causes and mechanism we know far too little, the most remarkable characteristic is the way in which the superego—you may call it, but in a whisper, the conscience—treats the ego. The melancholiac during periods of health can, like any one else, be more or less severe towards himself; but when he has a melancholic attack, his super-ego becomes over-severe, abuses, humiliates, and ill-treats his unfortunate ego, threatens it with the severest punishments, reproaches it for long forgotten actions which were at the time regarded quite lightly, and behaves as though it had spent the whole interval in amassing complaints and was only waiting for its present increase in strength to bring them forward, and to condemn the ego on their account. The super-ego has the ego at its mercy and applies the most severe moral standards to it . . . after a certain number of months the whole moral fuss is at an end, the critical voice of the super-ego is silent, the ego is reinstated, and enjoys once more all the rights of man until the next attack.

NILP—ch. 3

MEMORY

Memory, Concealment of—The formation of a concealing memory depends on the forgetting of other important impressions. In the case of forgetting of names, *we are aware* that the substitutive names are *incorrect,* while in concealing memories, we are surprised that we have them at all.
PEL—ch. 4

I particularly emphasized a peculiarity in the temporal relation between the concealing memory and the contents of the memory concealed by it. The content of the concealing memory in that example belonged to one of the first years of childhood, while the thoughts represented by it, which remained practically unconscious, belonged to a later period of the individual in question. I called this form of displacement a retro-active or *regressive* one. Perhaps more often, one finds the reversed relation—that is, an indifferent impression of the most remote period becomes a concealing memory in consciousness, which simply owes its existence to an association with an earlier experience, against whose direct reproduction there are resistances. We would call these *encroaching* or *interposing* concealing memories. What most concerns the memory lies here chronologically beyond the concealing memory. Finally, there may be a third possible case, namely, the concealing memory may be connected with the impression it conceals, not only through its contents, but also through contiguity of time; this is the *contemporaneous* or *contiguous* concealing memory.
PEL—ch. 4

Memory, Errors of—Errors of memory are distinguished from forgetting and false recollections through one feature only, namely, that the error (false recollection) is not recognized as such but finds credence. However, the use of the

expression "error" seems to depend on still another condition. We speak of "erring" instead of "falsely recollecting" where the character of the objective reality is emphasized in the psychic material to be reproduced—that is, where something other than a fact of my own psychic life is to be remembered, or rather something that may be confirmed or refuted through the memory of others. The reverse of the error in memory in this sense is formed by ignorance.
PEL—ch. 10

MENTAL LIFE—Psychoanalysis makes a basic assumption. . . . We assume that mental life is the function of an apparatus to which we ascribe the characteristics of being extended in space and of being made up of several portions—which we imagine, that is, as being like a telescope or microscope or something of the sort.
OoPA—ch. 1

Our mental life as a whole is governed by *three polarities*, namely, the following antitheses: Subject (ego)—Object (external world), Pleasure—Pain, Active—Passive.
I & V

MODESTY—Modesty, which is regarded as a feminine characteristic *par excellence*, but is far more a matter of convention than one would think, was, in our opinion, originally designed to hide the deficiency in her genitals.
NILP—ch. 5

MORALITY—Morality, of course, does not develop simultaneously in all its departments, and furthermore, the duration of the amoral period of childhood differs in different individuals. Where this morality fails to develop we are prone to speak of "degeneration"; but here the case is obviously one of arrested development. Where the primary character is already overlaid by the later development it may be at least partially uncovered again by an attack of hysteria. The correspondence between the so-called hysterical character and that of a naughty child is positively striking. The obsessional neurosis, on the other hand, corresponds to a super-morality, which develops as a strong reinforcement against the primary character that is threatening to revive. IoD—ch. 5

MOURNING—Mourning originates under the influence of reality testing, which demands categorically that one must part from the object because the object no longer exists. Now it is the task of mourning to carry out this retreat from the object in all the situations in which the object was the recipient of an intense cathexis. The painful character of this separation accords with the explanation just given—that is, it is explained by the intense and unrealizable longingful cathexis of the object during the reproduction of the situations in which the tie to the object has to be dissolved. PoA—ch. 11

N

NEURASTHENIA—On the one hand, we find cases in which definite symptoms characteristic of *neurasthenia* are conspicuous: cranial pressure, tendency to fatigue, dyspepsia, constipation, irritation of the spine, and so forth. On the other hand, in certain cases these indications are of minor importance and the syndrome is composed of other symptoms which all show a relation to one main symptom, to "anxiety" (free-floating anxiety, restlessness, expectant anxiety, complete, rudimentary or supplementary anxiety-attacks, locomotor vertigo, agoraphobia, sleeplessness, exacerbation of pains, etc.). I have left to the former type of neurasthenia its designation, but have distinguished the second as "anxiety-neurosis" both neuroses commonly appear together.
SAoN

NEUROSIS—Neurosis is the result of a conflict between the ego and its *id*.
N & P

The neurotic turns away from reality because he finds it unbearable—either the whole or parts of it.
FPMF

It is *quantitative disharmonies* that must be held responsible for the inadequacies and sufferings of neurotics. The determining causes of all the varying forms of human mental life are to be looked for in the interplay between inherited dispositions and accidental experiences.
OoPA—ch. 7

What did we regard as the essence of a neurosis? The fact that the Ego, the more highly organized part of the mental apparatus bred up under the influence of the outer world, is not in a position to fulfill its function of mediation between Id and reality; that in its weakness it retreats from some part of the instinctual activity of the Id; and suffers the consequences of this renunciation in the form of contractions of its influence, symptoms, and unsuccessful reaction-formations.
QLA—ch. 7

Neurosis seems to be a human privilege.
M & M—Part III, Section I

The neuroses have specific characteristics, they are misery of a particular sort.
OoPA—ch. 7

According to all that we know of the structure of the simpler neuroses of everyday life, it is very improbable that a neurosis should come about only by reason of the objective fact of exposure to danger without the participation of the deeper unconscious strata of the mental apparatus.
PoA—ch. 7

Defense against dangerous perceptions is a general task of neurosis.
PoA—ch. 10

It is indeed a universal characteristic of the neuroses that there are present in the subject's mental life, as regards some particular behavior, two different attitudes, contrary to each other and independent of each other; in that case,

however, one of them belongs to the ego and the opposing one, which is repressed, belongs to the id.
OoPA—ch. 8

Neurosis, Formation of—As a consequence of a certain experience there arises an instinctual demand which claims satisfaction. The ego foregoes this satisfaction, either because it is paralyzed by the excessiveness of the demand or because it recognizes in it a danger. The first of these reasons is the original one; both end in the avoidance of a dangerous situation. The Ego guards against this danger by repression. The excitation becomes inhibited in one way or another; the incitement, with the observations and perceptions belonging to it, is forgotten. This, however, does not bring the process to an end; either the instinct has kept its strength, or it will regain it, or it is reawakened by a new situation. It renews its claim and—since the way to normal satisfaction is barred by what we may call the scar tissue of repression—it gains at some weak point new access to a so-called substitutive satisfaction which now appears as a symptom, without the acquiescence and also without the comprehension of the Ego. All phenomena of symptom-formation can be fairly described as "the return of the repressed."
M & M—Part III, Section II

[Neurotic disturbance:] an Ego, prevented in its synthetizing activity, with no influence over a part of the Id, obliged to renounce some of its activities in order to avoid a fresh collision with what is repressed, exhausting itself in defense reactions—largely in vain—against the symptoms or derivatives of the repressed impulses; and an Id in which individual instincts have made themselves independent, pursuing their own aims without regard for the interests of the whole personality, and obeying only the laws of the primitive psychology which reigns in the depths of the Id. If we survey the whole situation it becomes clear that there is a simple formula for the arising of a neurosis; the Ego has made an attempt to suppress certain parts of the Id by an *inappropriate method*, and this has miscarried, and the Id has taken its revenge. Neurosis is thus the consequence of a conflict between Ego and Id, on which the Ego centers because—as further investigation shows—it insists throughout on retaining its adaptability towards the outer world. The opposition lies between outer world and Id, and because the Ego, true to its inmost nature, takes sides with the outer world, it becomes involved in conflict with its own Id. But mark well that it is not the fact of this conflict which brings about the illness—for such opposition between reality and Id is unavoidable, and the Ego's constant task is to mediate between them. It is the fact that the Ego, for settling the conflict, has employed the inadequate method of repression. But this in turn arises from the fact that at the time when this task was presented to it the Ego was undeveloped and weak. Decisive repressions all occur in early childhood.

QLA—ch. 3

Neurosis and Perversion—A great part of the opposition to these, my theories, is explained by the fact that the sexuality from which I deduce the psychoneurotic symptoms is thought of as coincident with the normal sexual instinct. But psychoanalysis teaches us more than that. It shows that the symptoms do not by any means result at the expense only of the so-called normal sexual instinct (at least not exclusively or preponderately), but they represent the converted expression of impulses which in a broader sense might be designated as *perverse* if they could manifest them-

selves directly in phantasies and acts without deviating from consciousness. The symptoms are, therefore, partially formed at the cost of abnormal sexuality. *The neurosis is, so to say, the negative of the perversion.*
TCTS I

Neurosis and Psychosis—The neuroses and psychoses are states in which disturbances in the functioning of the [psychical] apparatus come to expression.
OPA—ch. 7

Neurosis is the result of a conflict between the ego and its id, whereas psychosis is the analogous outcome of a similar disturbance in the relation between the ego and its environment (outer world).
N & P

Neurosis and psychosis are clearly intimately related, and yet at a decisive point they must separate. This point might well be that at which the Ego decides which side it will take. In both cases the Id would stick to its character of blind obduracy.
QLA—ch. 3

NEUROTICS—There is a class of psychological patients who evidently resemble the psychotics very closely, the immense number of sufferers from severe neuroses. The causes as well as the pathogenic mechanisms of their illness must be the same or at least very similar. Their ego, however, has proved more resistant and has become less disorganized. Many of them, in spite of their troubles and of their consequent inadequacy are none the less able to maintain their position in real life.
OoPA—ch. 6

There is no doubt that persons whom we call neurotic remain infantile in their attitude towards danger, and have not grown out of antiquated conditions for anxiety. Let us accept this as a factual contribution to our characterization of neurotics, why it should be so is not so easy to say.

NILP—ch. 4

Neurotics have approximately the same innate dispositions as other people, they have the same experiences and they have the same problems to solve.

OoPA—ch. 7

They complain of their illness, but they make the most of it, and when it comes to taking it away from them they will defend it like a lioness her young; there is no use in reproaching them with their contradiction.

QLA—ch. 5

It is very important for mental health that the Super-Ego should develop normally—that is, that it should become sufficiently depersonalized. It is precisely this that does not happen in the case of a neurotic, because his Œdipus complex does not undergo the right transformation. His Super-Ego deals with his Ego like a strict father with a child, and his idea of morality displays itself in primitive ways by making the Ego submit to punishment by the Super-Ego. Illness is employed as a means for this "self-punishment." The neurotic has to behave as though he were mastered by guilt, which the illness serves to punish, and so to relieve him.

QLA—ch. 5

O

OEDIPUS COMPLEX—*Œdipus complex, so* named because its essential substance is found in the Greek myth of King Œdipus, which has luckily been preserved for us in a version from the hand of a great dramatist. The Greek hero killed his father and married his mother. That he did so unknowingly, since he did not recognize them as his parents, constitutes a deviation from the analytical subject matter which is easily intelligible and indeed inevitable.
OoPA—ch. 7

Castration has a place, too, in the Œdipus legend, for the blinding with which Œdipus punished himself after the discovery of his crime is, by the evidence of dreams, a symbolic substitute for castration.
OoPA—ch. 7

Oedipus Complex in Women—With the transference of the child-penis wish on to her father, the girl enters into the situation of the Œdipus-complex. The hostility against her mother, which did not require to be newly created, now receives a great reinforcement, for her mother becomes a rival, who gets everything from her father that she herself

wants. The girl's Œdipus-complex has long concealed from us the pre-œdipal attachment to her mother which is so important and which leaves behind it such lasting fixations. For the girl, the Œdipus situation is the conclusion of a long and difficult period of development, it is a kind of temporary solution of her problem, a state of equilibrium which is not lightly to be given up, especially as the onset of the latency period is not far off. And here we notice a difference between the two sexes in the relation between the Œdipus-complex and the castration-complex, a difference which is probably a momentous one. The boy's Œdipus-complex, in which he desires his mother, and wants to get rid of his father as a rival, develops naturally out of the phase of phallic sexuality. The threat of castration, however, forces him to give up this attitude. Under the influence of the danger of losing his penis, he abandons his Œdipus-complex; it is repressed and in the most normal cases entirely destroyed, while a severe super-ego is set up as its heir. What happens in the case of the girl is almost the opposite. The castration-complex prepares the way for the Œdipus-complex instead of destroying it; under the influence of her penis-envy the girl is driven from her attachment to her mother, and enters the Œdipus situation, as though it were a haven of refuge. When the fear of castration disappears, the primary motive is removed, which has forced the boy to overcome his Œdipus-complex. The girl remains in the Œdipus situation for an indefinite period, she only abandons it late in life, and then incompletely. The formation of the super-ego must suffer in these circumstances.
NILP—ch. 5

OEDIPUS LEGEND—In the very text of Sophocles' tragedy there is an unmistakable reference to the fact that

the Œdipus legend had its source in dream-material of im-
memorial antiquity, the content of which was the painful
disturbance of the child's relations to its parents caused by
the first impulses of sexuality.
IoD—ch. 5

P

PAIN—Most of the "pain" we experience is of a perceptual order, perception either of the urge of unsatisfied instincts or of something in the external world which may be painful in itself or may arouse painful anticipations in the psychic apparatus and is recognized by it as "danger."
BPP—ch. 1

Pain, Physical—Pain—primarily and as a rule—occurs if a stimulus impinging on the periphery breaks through the defenses that oppose stimuli of excessive strength and hence acts like a continuous instinctual stimulus against which otherwise efficacious muscular activity such as serves to remove the stimulated region from the stimulus remains powerless. If the pain does not originate from a point on the skin but from an internal organ, this does not alter the situation in any way; it is only that a bit of the internal periphery has replaced the external. . . . In the case of physical pain there arises an intense cathexis, which may be termed narcissistic, of the painful region of the body—a cathexis which increases progressively and which acts upon the ego in a so to speak evacuative manner.
PoA—ch. 11

Pain, Psychic—It certainly cannot be without significance that language has created the concept of inward, of psychic, pain, and has equated the sensations attendant upon object loss with physical pain.
PoA—ch. 11

PARANOIA—On the basis of [certain] clinical evidence we can suppose that paranoiacs are endowed with a *fixation at the stage of narcissism,* and we can assert that the amount of *regression* characteristic of paranoia is indicated by the length of *the step back from sublimated homosexuality to narcissism.*
ParDP—ch. 3

Many things obtrude themselves on consciousness in paranoia, which in normal and neurotic persons can only be demonstrated through psychoanalysis as existing in their unconscious. (For example, the phantasies of the hysterical regarding sexual and cruel abuse which are made conscious by analysis often correspond in every detail with the complaints of persecuted paranoiacs. It is remarkable, but not altogether unexpected that we also meet the identical content as reality in the contrivances of perverts for the gratification of their desires.)
PEL—ch. 10

PARAPHRENIA—It would seem to me the most convenient plan to give dementia praecox the name of *paraphrenia.* This term has no special connotation, and it would serve to indicate a relationship with paranoia (a name which may be regarded as fixed) and would further recall hebephrenia, an entity which is now merged in dementia praecox.
ParDP—ch. 3

Patients suffering from dementia praecox or schizophre-

nia whom I propose to term paraphrenics display two fundamental characteristics: They suffer from megalomania and they have withdrawn their interest from the external world (people and things).
Narc

The libido that is liberated by frustration does not remain attached to objects in phantasy, but returns to the ego; the megalomania then represents the mastery of this volume of libido, and thus corresponds with the introversion on to the phantasy-creations that is found in the transference neuroses; the hypochondria of paraphrenia, which is homologous to the anxiety of the transference neuroses, arises from a failure of this effort in the mental apparatus.
Narc

PARENTS

Father—I could not point to any need in childhood so strong as that for a father's protection.
C & D—ch. 1

The idea of being eaten by the father belongs to the typical primal stock of childhood ideas; analogies from mythology (Kronos) and from animal life are generally familiar.
PoA—ch. 4

Father-Fixation (in Women)—We have made the most surprising discoveries about these women who display intense and prolonged father-fixations. We knew, of course, that there had been an earlier stage in which they were attached to their mother; but we did not know that it was so rich in content, that it persisted so long, and that it could leave behind it so many occasions for fixations and predispositions. During this time, their father is no more than an irksome rival. In many cases the attachment to the mother lasts beyond the fourth year; almost everything that we find later in the father-relation was already present in that attachment, and has been subsequently transferred on to the father. In short, we gain the conviction that one cannot understand women, unless one estimates this *pre-œdipal attachment to the mother* at its proper value.

NILP—ch. 5

Mother—A child's first erotic object is the mother's breast that feeds him, and love in its beginnings attaches itself to the satisfaction of the need for food. To start with, the child certainly makes no distinction between the breast and his own body, when the breast has to be separated from his body and shifted to the "outside" because he so often finds it absent, it carries with it, now that it is an *"object,"* part of the original narcissistic cathexis. This first object subsequently becomes completed into the whole person of the child's mother, who not only feeds him but also looks after him and thus arouses in him many other physical sensations pleasant and unpleasant. By her care of the child's body she becomes his first seducer. In these two relations lies the root of a mother's importance, unique, without parallel, laid down unalterably for a whole lifetime, as the first and strongest love-object and as the prototype of all later love relations—for both sexes. The phylogenetic foundation has so much the upper hand in all this over accidental personal experience that it makes no difference whether a child has really sucked at the breast or has been brought up on the bottle and never enjoyed the tenderness of a mother's care. His development takes the same path in both cases; it may be that in the latter event his later longing is all the greater. And for however long a child is fed at his mother's breast, he will always be left with a conviction after he is weaned that his feeding was too short and too little.

OoPA—ch. 7

PERVERSION—We have been forced to perceive in every fixed aberration from the normal sexual life, a fragment of inhibited development and infantilism. . . . The perversions thus prove themselves to be, on the one hand, inhibitions, and on the other, dissociations from the normal development.
TCTS III

The union of the genitals in the characteristic act of copulation is taken as the normal sexual aim. . . . Yet, even in the most normal sexual act, certain addenda are distinguishable, the development of which may lead to aberrations described as *perversions*. . . . The perversions represent either (a) anatomical *transgressions* of the bodily regions destined for sexual union, or (b) a *lingering* at the intermediary relations to the sexual object which should normally be rapidly passed, on the way to the definite sexual aim.
TCTS I

See also *Neurosis* and *Perversion*.

Sadism and Masochism as Perversions—We use the word "sadism" when sexual satisfaction depends upon the sexual object suffering pain, ill-treatment and humiliation, and the word "masochism," when the subject himself has to suffer such treatment. You know, too, that there is a certain admixture of these two tendencies in normal sexual relations, and that we call them "perversions" when they thrust the other sexual aims into the background, and substitute their own aims for them.
NILP—ch. 4

PERVERT—There are people whose desires behave in every way like sexual ones, but who at the same time entirely disregard the sexual organs or their normal use; people of this kind are known as "perverts."
OoPA—ch. 3

PHOBIA—We have in the phobias, after all, merely the substituting of one external danger for another. The fact that in phobias the ego is able to escape anxiety through a process of avoidance or by means of an inhibition is in complete accord with the concept that this anxiety is simply an affective signal, and that with regard to the economic situation involved nothing has been altered.
PoA—ch. 7

Among the phobias two groups may be differentiated, according to the nature of the object feared: (1) common phobias, an exaggerated fear of all those things that everyone detests or fears to some extent: such as night, solitude, death, illness, dangers in general, snakes, etc.; (2) specific phobias, the fear of special circumstances that inspire no fear in the normal man; for example, agoraphobia and the other phobias of locomotion.
O & P

Phobias of Early Childhood—The enigmatic phobias of early childhood deserve mention once again. Certain of them—the fear of being alone, of the dark, of strangers—we can understand as reactions to the danger of object loss; with regard to others—fear of small animals, thunderstorms, etc.—there is the possibility that they represent the atrophied remnants of an innate preparedness against reality dangers such as is so well developed in other animals. It is the part of this archaic heritage having to do with object loss which alone has utility for man. If such childhood phobias become fixed, grow more intense, and persist into a later period of life, analysis demonstrates that their content has become connected with instinctual demands, has become the representative of internal dangers also.
PoA—ch. 11

Phobia and Sexual Life—the main point in the problem of phobias seems to me that *phobias do not occur at all when the vita sexualis is normal.*
RCA-N

PRECONSCIOUS—Everything unconscious that can easily exchange the unconscious condition for the conscious one, is better described as "capable of entering consciousness," or as *preconscious.*
OoPA—ch. 4

From a purely descriptive point of view, the "preconscious' is also unconscious, but we do not give it that name, except when we are speaking loosely, or when we have to defend in general the existence of unconscious processes in mental life.
NILP—ch. 3

That which is latent, and only unconscious in the descriptive and not in the dynamic sense, we call *preconscious;* the term unconscious we reserve for the dynamically unconscious repressed, so that we now have three terms, conscious (Cs), preconscious (Pcs), and unconscious (Ucs), which are no longer purely descriptive in sense.
E & I—ch. 1

PSYCHIATRY—Psychiatry, alone, is concerned with the disturbances of mental functioning; but one knows in what way and with what purposes. Psychiatry looks for the physical causes of mental disorders and treats them like those of any other illness.
QLA—ch. 6

PSYCHOANALYSIS [cf. also ANALYSIS]—Psychoanalysis is the name (1) of a procedure for the investigation of mental processes which are almost inaccessible in any other way, (2) of a method (based upon that investigation) for the treatment of neurotic disorders and (3) of a collection of psychological information obtained along those lines, which is gradually being accumulated into a new scientific discipline.

PA

Psychoanalysis is a dynamic conception, which reduces mental life to the interplay of reciprocally urging and checking forces.

PVD

The contribution of psychoanalysis to science consists precisely in having extended research to the region of the mind.

NILP—ch. 7

Psychoanalysis is not, in my opinion, in a position to create a *Weltanschauung* of its own. It has no need to do so, for it is a branch of science, and can subscribe to the scientific *Weltanschauung*.

NILP—ch. 7

Psychoanalysis, Field of Application of—The field in which analytical therapy can be applied is that of the transference-neuroses, phobias, hysterias, obsessional neuroses, and besides these such abnormalities of character as have been developed instead of these diseases. Everything other than these, such as narcissistic or psychotic conditions, is more or less unsuitable.

NILP—ch. 6

The sphere of application of psychoanalysis extends as far as that of psychology, to which it forms a complement of the greatest moment.

ABS—ch. 6

The impulses and their transformations are the last

things psychoanalysis can discern. Henceforth it leaves the
stage to biological investigation.
LVD—ch. 6

Psychoanalysis, Objects and Aims of—The analysis aims
at laying bare the complexes which have been repressed as
a result of the painful feelings associated with them, and
which produce signs of resistance when there is an attempt
to bring them into consciousness.
PA & CL

It is one of the tasks of psychoanalysis to lift the veil of
amnesia which shrouds the earliest years of childhood and
to bring the expressions of infantile sexual life which are
hidden behind it into conscious memory.
NILP—ch. 1

Psychoanalysis, Theory of—The whole of psychoanalytic
theory is in fact built up on the perception of the resistance
exerted by the patient when we try to make him conscious
of his unconscious.
NILP—ch. 3

Psychoanalysis as a Therapeutic Method—One of the first
applications of psychoanalysis was that we were able to understand the opposition we had to meet on account of our
psychoanalytic activities. . . . Psychoanalysis originated as a
therapeutic procedure; it has gone far beyond that, but it
has never given up its original field of work, and it still re-
lies upon contact with clinical material for its further advances and development. The accumulation of empirical
data upon which we base our theories can be obtained in no
other way. . . . Psychoanalysis really is a form of therapy,
just as other methods are. . . . As a psychotherapeutic

method, analysis does not stand in opposition to other methods employed in this branch of medicine; it does not invalidate them nor does it exclude them. . . . The practice of psychoanalysis is difficult and exacting! . . . As a rule psychoanalysis either possesses the doctor entirely or not at all. . . . Compared with other psychotherapeutic procedures, psychoanalysis is far and away the most powerful.

PSYCHOSIS—In psychoses, the turning away from reality is brought about in two ways; either because the repressed unconscious is too strong, so that it overwhelms the conscious which tries to cling on to reality, or because reality has become so unbearably painful that the threatened ego, in a despairing gesture of opposition, throws itself into the arms of the unconscious impulses.
NILP—ch. 1

PUBERTY—The complete organization [of sexuality] is not attained until puberty, in a fourth, or genital, phase. A state of affairs is then established in which (1) many earlier libidinal cathexes are retained, (2) others are included in the sexual function as preparatory or auxiliary acts, their satisfaction producing what is known as fore-pleasure, and (3) other tendencies are excluded from the organization, and are either entirely suppressed (repressed) or are employed in the ego in some other way, forming character-traits or undergoing sublimation with a displacement of their aims.
OoPA—ch. 3

Puberty forms a definite epoch in the development of the compulsion neurosis. The genital organization, interrupted in childhood, is now resumed with great vigor.
PoA—ch. 5

Q

QUACK—In the eyes of the law, a quack is one who treats patients without being able to produce a State medical degree. I should prefer another definition: a quack is a person who undertakes a treatment without possessing the knowledge and capacity required for it.
QLA—ch. 6

R

REGRESSION—As to the regression, we may further observe that it plays a no less important part in the theory of neurotic symptom-formation than in the theory of dreams. We may therefore distinguish a threefold species of regression: *(a)* a *topical* one, in the sense of the scheme of the Ψ-systems here expounded; *(b)* a *temporal* one, in so far as it is a regression to older psychic formations; and *(c)* a *formal* one, when primitive modes of expression and representation take the place of the customary modes. These three forms of regression are, however, basically one, and in the majority of cases they coincide, for that which is older in point of time is at the same time formally primitive and, in the psychic topography, nearer to the perception-end.
IoD—ch. 7

Regression in Dreams—In regression the structure of the dream-thoughts breaks up into its raw material.
IoD—ch. 7

Regression of Instinctual Impulses—In compulsion neurosis there is brought about, under the influence of the ego's opposition, a regression of the instinctual impulses to an

earlier libidinal phase such as does not, it is true, make repression superfluous, but evidently operates to the same effect as repression.
PoA—ch. 11

Regression, Temporal—When we investigate psychoneurotic conditions, we find in each of them occasion to com-
ment upon a so-called *temporal regression, i.e.* the particular
extent to which each of them retraces the stages of its evolution. We distinguish two such regressions—one in the development of the ego and the other in that of the libido. In
sleep, the latter is carried to the point of restoring the primitive narcissism, while the former goes back to the state of
hallucinatory wish-fulfilment.
MSTD

RELIGION—The derivation of a need for religion from the
child's feeling of helplessness and the longing it evokes for
a father seems to me incontrovertible, especially since this
feeling is not simply carried on from childhood days but is
kept alive perpetually by the fear of what the superior
power of fate will bring.
C & D—ch. 1

Religion is an attempt to get control over the sensory
world, in which we are placed, by means of the wish-world
which we have developed inside us as a result of biological
and psychological necessities. But it cannot achieve its end.
Its doctrines carry with them the stamp of the times in
which they originated, the ignorant childhood days of the
human race. Its consolations deserve no trust. . . . If one at-
tempts to assign to religion its place in man's evolution, it
seems not so much to be a lasting acquisition, as a parallel
to the neurosis which the civilized individual must pass
through on his way from childhood to maturity.
NILP—ch. 7

Religion and Neurosis—Religious phenomena are to be understood only on the model of the neurotic symptoms of the individual, which are so familiar to us, as a return of long-forgotten important happenings in the primeval history of the human family, that they owe their obsessive character to that very origin and therefore derive their effect on mankind from the historical truth they contain.

M & M—Part III, Section II

One might venture to regard the obsessional neurosis as a pathological counterpart to the formation of a religion, to describe this neurosis as a private religious system, and religion as a universal obsessional neurosis.

OA & RL

It is easy to see wherein lies the resemblance between neurotic ceremonial and religious rites; it is in the fear of pangs of conscience after their omission, in the complete isolation of them from all other activities (the feeling that one must not be disturbed), and in the conscientiousness with which the details are carried out.

OA & RL

REMORSE—Remorse is a general term denoting the ego's reaction under a special form of the sense of guilt; it includes the almost unaltered sensory material belonging to the anxiety that is at work behind the sense of guilt; it is itself a punishment; it too, therefore, may occur before conscience has developed.

C & D—ch. 8

RENUNCIATION, INSTINCTUAL—When the Id makes an instinctual demand of an erotic or aggressive nature on a human being, the most simple and natural response for the Ego, which governs the apparatus for thinking and muscle innervation, is to satisfy this by an action. This satisfaction

of the instinct is felt as pleasure by the Ego, just as not satis-
fying this instinct would undoubtedly become a source of
discomfort. Now, it may happen that the Ego eschews satisfaction of the instinct because of external obstacles—
namely, when it realizes that the action in question would
bring in its course serious danger to the Ego. Such a refrain-
ing from satisfaction, an "instinctual renunciation" because
of external obstacles—as we say, in obedience to the reality-
principle—is never pleasurable. The instinctual renunciation would bring about a lasting painful tension if we did
not succeed in diminishing the strength of the instinctual
urge itself through a displacement of energy. This instinctual renunciation may also be forced on us, however, by
other motives, which we rightly call inner ones. In the
course of individual development a part of the inhibiting
forces in the outer world becomes internalized; a standard
is created in the Ego which opposes the other faculties by
observation, criticism, and prohibition. We call this new
standard the *Super-ego*. . . . While, however, instinctual renunciation for external reasons is only painful, renunciation
for internal reasons, in obedience to the demands of the
Super-ego, has another economic effect. It brings besides
the inevitable pain a gain in pleasure to the Ego—as it were,
a substitutive satisfaction.
M & M—Part III, Section II

REPRESSION—The infantile ego, under the domination of
the external world, disposes of undesirable instinctual demands by means of what are called repressions.
OoPA—ch. 8

   The essence of repression lies simply in the function of
rejecting and keeping something out of consciousness.
Repr

   The theory of repression became the foundation-stone of

our understanding of the neuroses. . . . It is possible to take repression as a centre and to bring all the elements of psychoanalytical theory into relation with it.
ABS—ch. 3

Repression takes place in two distinct situations, namely, when an unwelcome instinctual impulse is aroused by an external perception, and when the impulse arises internally without such provocation.
PoA—ch. 2

Decisive repressions all occur in early childhood.
QLA—ch. 3

Repression . . . is, at bottom, an attempt at flight.
PoA—ch 10

The Ego feels a demand from an instinct which it wishes to withstand, because it suspects that satisfaction is dangerous, would evoke a traumatic situation, a collision with the outer world; but it cannot master it, because it has not yet the strength necessary. The Ego then treats the risk from the instinct as though it were an outside danger, and makes an attempt at flight; it withdraws from that part of the Id, leaving it to its fate, after having refused it all the help which it normally affords to instinctual impulses. We put it, that Ego undertakes a *repression* of these instinctual impulses. By the act of repression the Ego follows the pleasure principle, which otherwise it is wont to correct, and it suffers harm on this account. The harm consists in the fact that the Ego has now imposed a lasting limitation on its sphere of power. The repressed instinctual impulse is henceforth isolated; it is left to itself and inaccessible, but this means that it cannot be influenced. It goes its own way.
QLA—ch. 3

Repression proceeds from the ego, which, possibly at the command of the superego, does not wish to be a party to an instinct cathexis originating in the id. Through repression

the ego accomplishes the exclusion from consciousness of the idea which was the carrier of the unwelcome impulse. Analysis frequently demonstrates that the idea has been retained as an unconscious formation.
PoA—ch. 2

It is an important element of the theory of repression that this process is not one which takes place on a single occasion but is one demanding a continuous expenditure of effort.
PoA—ch. 10

Repression, Ego and—As I understand it, in repression the ego functions under the influence of external reality and therefore excludes the result of the substitutive process from this reality.

The ego controls the entrance into consciousness as well as the passage into activity directed to the environment; in repression it exerts its power at both places. The instinct representative experiences the one, the instinctual impulse itself the other side of the ego's manifestation of authority.
PoA—ch. 2

Repression, Ego and Id and—In the case of repression the fact of crucial importance is that the ego is an organized entity, whereas the id is not; in fact, the ego is the organized part of the id. It would be quite unjustifiable to conceive of the ego and the id as if they were two opposing camps—as though through repression the ego were seeking to suppress a part of the id, and that thereupon the rest of the id came to the assistance of the part attacked and measured its strength against that of the ego.
PoA—ch. 3

Repression, Primal—The majority of repressions with which we have to do in therapeutic work are instances of *subse-*

quential repression. They presuppose *primal* repressions of an earlier date which exercise over the more recent situation their gravitative influence.

PoA—ch. 2

Repression, Superego and—Now we have posited a special function within the ego to represent the demand for restriction and rejection, *i.e.* the super-ego, we can say that repression is the work of the super-ego,—either that it does its work on its own account or else that the ego does it in obedience to its orders.

NILP—ch. 3

Repression, Tendency to—The tendency to repression . . . must be traced back to the organic bases of the character, upon which alone the psychic structure rises.

LDV—ch. 6

REPRESSION-RESISTANCE—Ego's repression-resistance (that is, the unpleasure felt by it at undertaking the severe work imposed upon it).

OoPA—ch. 6

The ego protects itself against the incursion of undesirable elements from the unconscious and repressed id by means of anti-cathexes, which must remain intact if it is to function normally. The more hardly the ego feels itself pressed, the more convulsively it clings (in terror, as it were) to these anticathexes, in order to protect what remains of it from further irruptions. . . . The ego shrinks from undertakings that seem dangerous and threaten unpleasure; it must be constantly spurred on and soothed down if it is not to fail us. This resistance, which persists through the whole treatment and is renewed with every fresh piece

of work, has been named, though not quite correctly, *repression-resistance*.
OoPA—ch. 6

RESISTANCE IN ANALYSIS—The whole of psychoanalytic theory is in fact built up on the perception of the resistance exerted by the patient when we try to make him conscious of his unconscious. The objective indication of resistance is that his associations stop short or wander far away from the theme that is being discussed. He may also become subjectively aware of the resistance by experiencing painful feelings when he approaches the theme. But this last indication may be absent.
NILP—ch. 3

We call all the forces which oppose the work of cure the patient's "resistances." The gain from the illness is the source of one resistance, and "unconscious guilt" represents the resistance from the Super-Ego; this is the most powerful factor, and the one we most fear. We meet still other resistances in the course of the treatment. If the Ego, in the early period, undertook a repression on account of anxiety, that anxiety still exists, and now expresses itself as a resistance if the Ego approaches what is repressed. It may well be imagined that difficulties arise when an instinctual process, which has followed a certain path perhaps for decades, is suddenly required to take a new course which has now opened for it. One might call that the resistance of the Id. The fight against all these resistances is the main work in the treatment, and the task of interpretation seems small beside it.
QLA—ch. 4

The overcoming of resistance is the part of our work which requires the greatest time and the greatest trouble.
OoPA—ch. 6

The fifth type of resistance . . . of the superego, the last recognized and the most obscure, but not always the weakest, seems to derive from the sense of guilt or need of punishment; it resists any success and hence also recovery through the analysis.

PoA—ch. 11

S

SADISM—The roots of active algolagnia, sadism, can be readily demonstrable in the normal individual. The sexuality of most men shows an admixture of aggression, of a desire to subdue, the biological significance of which lies in the necessity for overcoming the resistance of the sexual object by actions other than mere *courting*. Sadism would then correspond to an aggressive component of the sexual instinct which has become independent and exaggerated and has been brought to the foreground by displacement.

The concept of sadism fluctuates in everyday speech from a mere active or impetuous attitude towards the sexual object to an absolute attachment of the gratification to the subjection and maltreatment of the object. Strictly speaking, only the last extreme case can claim the name of perversion.
TCTS I

SCIENCE—Scientific thought is, in its essence, no different from the normal process of thinking, which we all, believers and unbelievers, alike, make use of when we are going about our business in everyday life. . . . Its aim is to arrive at correspondence with reality, that is to say with what exists

outside us and independently of us, and, as experience has taught us, is decisive for the fulfilment or frustration of our desires. This correspondence with the real external world we call truth.
NILP—ch. 7

SCREEN-MEMORY—The period of infantile amnesia is often interrupted by isolated fragmentary memories, the so-called "screen-memories."
M & M—Part III, Section I

"SELF-ANALYSIS"—We consider that everyone who wishes to treat others by analysis should first undergo an analysis himself. Only in the course of this "self-analysis" (as it is mistakenly termed), when he actually experiences in his own person, or rather in his own psyche, the processes asserted by analysis to take place, does he acquire the convictions by which he will be later guided as an analyst.
QLA—ch. 2

SEX ACT—The union of the genitals in the characteristic act of copulation is taken as the normal sexual aim. It serves to diminish the sexual tension and to quench temporarily the sexual desire (gratification analogous to satisfaction of hunger). Yet, even in the most normal sexual act, certain addenda are distinguishable, the development of which may lead to aberrations described as *perversions*.
TCTS I
   The execution of the sex act presupposes a very complicated sequence of events, any one of which may be the locus of disturbance.
PoA—ch. 1

SEXUAL AIM—The aim towards which the [sexual] instinct strives.
TCTS I

Sexual Aim, Infantile—Consists in the production of gratification through the proper excitation of this or that selected erogenous zone
TCTS II

SEXUAL EXCITEMENT—Sexual excitement is the expression of libidinal instinctual impulses.
PoA—ch. 4

SEXUAL FUNCTION, IMPAIRMENT OF—The most varied means are employed to impair function, as: (1) the mere turning aside of libido, which seems most easily to produce what we call pure inhibition; (2) impairment of the execution of the function; (3) the rendering it difficult through the imposition of special conditions, and its modification through diverting it to other aims; (4) its prevention by means of precautionary measures; (5) its discontinuance by the development of anxiety, when the initiation of the function can no longer be prevented; finally, (6) a subsequent reaction of protest against the act and a desire to undo it if it has actually been carried out.
PoA—ch. 1

SEXUAL IMPULSES—Observation of daily life shows us that most persons have the capacity to direct a very tangible part of their sexual motive powers to their professional or business activities. The sexual impulse is particularly suited to yield such contributions because it is endowed with the capacity of sublimation, i.e., it has the power to exchange its

nearest aim for others of higher value which are not sexual. We consider this process as proved, if the history of childhood or the history of the psychic development of a person shows that in his childhood this powerful impulse was in the service of sexual interest. We consider it a further corroboration if the sexual life of mature years evinces a striking stunting, as if a part of the sexual activity had now been replaced by the activity of the predominant impulse.
LDV—ch. 1

Most of the impulses of sexual life are not of a purely erotic nature but arise from alloys of the erotic instinct with components of the destructive instinct.
OoPA—ch. 7

SEXUAL INSTINCT AND LIBIDO—The fact of sexual need in man and animal is expressed in biology by the assumption of a "sexual instinct." This instinct is made analogous to the instinct of taking nourishment, and to hunger. The sexual expression corresponding to hunger not being found colloquially, science uses the expression, "libido."
TCTS I

SEXUAL LIFE—The sexual life of the human being does not develop in progressive fashion from incipience to maturity, as in the case of most of the closely related animals, but it suffers an abrupt interruption after an initial early florescence extending to about the fifth year, after which it commences anew with puberty, dovetailing, as it were, with the tendencies of the infantile period.
PoA—ch. 10

Sexual Life and Civilization—The sexual life of civilized man is seriously disabled, whatever we may say; it sometimes makes an impression of being a function in process of becoming atrophied, just as organs like our teeth and our hair seem to be.

C & D—ch. 4

Sexual Life and Phobia—Phobias do not occur at all when the vita sexualis is normal.

RCA-N

SEXUAL OBJECT—The person from whom the sexual attraction emanates.

TCTS I

Sexual Object, Unfit Substitutes for—We are especially impressed by those cases in which the normal sexual object is substituted for another, which, though related to it, is totally unfit for the normal sexual aim.

The substitute for the sexual object is generally a part of the body but little adapted for sexual purposes, such as the foot or hair or some inanimate object (fragments of clothing, underwear), which has some demonstrable relation to the sexual person, preferably to the sexuality of the same. This substitute is not unjustly compared with the fetish in which the savage sees the embodiment of his god.

The case becomes pathological only when the striving for the fetish fixes itself beyond such determinations and takes the place of the normal sexual aim; or again, when the fetish disengages itself from the person concerned and itself becomes a sexual object. These are the general determinants for the transition of mere variations of the sexual instinct to pathological aberrations.

TCTS I

SEXUALITY—Among the causes of and occasions for neurotic complaints sexual factors play an important, an overweening—even perhaps a specific—rôle.
QLA—ch. 4

Sexual life does not begin only at puberty, but starts with clear manifestations soon after birth.

It is necessary to distinguish sharply between the concepts of "sexual" and "genital." The former is the wider concept and includes many activities that have nothing to do with the genitals.

Sexual life comprises the function of obtaining pleasure from zones of the body—a function which is subsequently brought into the service of that of reproduction. The two functions often fail to coincide completely.
OoPA—ch. 3

Sexuality, Female—There can be no doubt that the bisexual disposition which we maintain to be characteristic of human beings manifests itself much more plainly in the female than in the male. The latter has only one principal sexual zone—only one sexual organ—whereas the former has two: the vagina, the true female organ, and the clitoris, which is analogous to the male organ. We believe that we may justly assume that for many years the vagina is virtually non-existent and possibly remains without sensation until puberty.
FS

Sexuality in Childhood—The sexual instinctual impulses accompany life from birth, and it is just these instincts against which the infantile Ego undertakes defense by repressions.
QLA—ch. 4

The child brings along into the world germs of sexual activity and even while taking nourishment, it at the same time also enjoys a sexual gratification which it then seeks again to procure for itself through the familiar activity of "thumb-sucking." The sexual activity of the child, however, does not develop in the same measure as his other functions, but merges first into the so-called latency period from the age of three to the age of five years. The production of sexual excitation by no means ceases at this period but continues to furnish a stock of energy, the greater part of which is utilized for aims other than sexual. On the one hand, it is used for the delivery of sexual components for social feelings, and on the other hand (by means of repression and reaction formation), for the erection of the future sex barriers. Accordingly, the forces which are destined to hold the sexual instinct in certain tracks are built up in infancy with the help of education at the expense of the greater part of the perverse sexual feelings. Another part of the infantile sexual manifestations escapes this utilization and may manifest itself as sexual activity. It can then be discovered that the sexual excitation of the child flows from diverse sources. Above all, gratifications originate through the adapted sensible excitation of so-called erogenous zones. For these probably any skin region or sensory organ may serve; but there are certain distinguished erogenous zones, the excitation of which by certain organic mechanisms, is assured from the beginning. Moreover, sexual excitation originates in the organism, as it were, as a by-product in a greater number of processes, as soon as they attain a certain intensity; this especially takes place in all strong emotional excitements, even if they be of a painful nature. The excitations from all these sources do not yet unite, but they pursue their aim individually—this aim consisting merely in

the gaining of a certain pleasure. The sexual instinct of childhood is therefore objectless or *autoerotic*.
TCTS III

A child's sexual life is naturally different from that of an adult. The sexual function undergoes a complicated development between its beginnings and the final form which we recognize as familiar. It grows together out of a number of component instincts with special aims, and passes through several phases of organization, until finally it is brought into the service of reproduction. The individual component-instincts are not all equally useful for the final purpose, and they must be diverted, remodelled, and in part suppressed. Such a far-reaching development is not always faultlessly carried out, and there may be inhibitions of development and partial fixations at early stages; where, later, the exercise of the sexual function is met by hindrances, the sexual striving—the libido, as we say—reverts to such earlier points of fixation. The study of childhood sexuality, and its changes on the way to maturity, has also given us the key to the understanding of the so-called sexual perversions.
QLA—ch. 4

The most remarkable feature—as it seems to me—in children's sexual life is that it runs its whole far-reaching course in the first five years of life. From then on, until puberty, it goes through the so-called latency period, in which, normally, sexuality makes no progress; on the contrary, the sexual strivings diminish in strength, and much that the child practiced or knew before is given up and forgotten. In this period, after the early blooming of sexual life has withered, are built up such attitudes of the Ego as shame, disgust, and morality, destined to stand against the later storms of puberty and to direct the paths of the freshly-awakened sexual

desires. This so-called *double onset of sexual life* has much to do with the rise of neurotic ailments.
QLA—ch. 4

A further characteristic of the sexuality of early child-hood is that the female organ as yet plays no part in it—the child has not yet discovered it. All the accent falls on the male organ, and all interest is concentrated on whether it is present or not.
QLA—ch. 4

A child's sexual impulses find their main outlet in gratifi-cation on its own body, by stimulation of its own genitals—in actual fact, the male component of the genitals.
QLA—ch. 4

.... psychoanalytic investigation ... teaches us that many, perhaps most, children, at least the most gifted ones, go through a period beginning with the third year, which may be designated as the period of *infantile sexual investiga-tion*. As far as we know, this curiosity is not awakened spontaneously in children of this age. It is aroused through the impression of an important experience, through the birth of a little brother or sister, or through fear of the same engendered by some outward experience, wherein the child sees a danger to his egotistic interests. The investigation di-rects itself to the question whence children come, as if the child were looking for means to guard against such an un-desired event. ... If the period of infantile sexual investiga-tion comes to an end through an impetus of energetic sexual repression, the early association with sexual interest may result in three different possibilities for the future fate of the investigation impulse. The investigation either shares the fate of the sexuality; the curiosity henceforth remains inhibited and the free activity of intelligence may become narrowed for life. This is especially favored shortly there-after by education and powerful religious inhibitions. This is the type of neurotic inhibition. . . . In a second type the intellectual development is sufficiently strong to withstand the sexual repression pulling at it. Sometimes, after the disappearance of the infantile sexual investigation, it offers its support to the old association in order to elude sexual repression, and the suppressed sexual investigation comes back from the unconscious as compulsive reasoning. It is naturally distorted and not free, but forceful enough to sexualize even thought itself and to accentuate the intellectual operations with the pleasure and anxiety of the actual sexual processes. Here the investigation becomes sexual activity and often exclusively so; the feeling of settling the problem and of explaining things in the mind is put in place of sexual gratification. But the indeterminate character of the infantile investigation repeats itself also in the fact that this reasoning never ends, and that the desired intellectual feeling of the solution constantly recedes into the distance.

By virtue of a special disposition the third, which is the most rare and most perfect type, escapes the inhibition of thought and the compulsive reasoning. Also here sexual repression takes place, but it does not succeed in evincing a partial impulse of the sexual pleasure in the unconscious; instead the libido withdraws from the fate of the repression by being sublimated from the outset into curiosity, and by reinforcing the powerful investigation impulse.
LDV—ch. 1

What attitude ought we to take towards the sexual indulgence of early childhood? We have become aware of the responsibility we incur by suppressing it, and yet we cannot assume that it is right to allow it unchecked. It appears that among races of low culture, and in the lower strata of civilized peoples, children's sexuality is allowed free play. That probably constitutes a strong protection against later lapses into individual neurosis, but is there not at the same time

great detriment to the aptitude for cultural achievement?
There is a good deal which goes to suggest that in this re-
spect we are between a new Scylla and Charybdis.
QLA—ch. 4

Second Phase of Childhood Masturbation. Infantile masturbation seems to disappear after a brief time, but it may continue uninterruptedly till puberty and thus represent the
first marked deviation from that development which is de-
sirable for civilized man. At some time during childhood
after the nursing period, the sexual instinct of the genitals
re-awakens and continues active for some time until it is
again suppressed, or it may continue without interruption.
TCTS II

Sexuality in Puberty—With the beginning of puberty,
changes set in, which transform the infantile sexual life into
its definite normal form. Hitherto, the sexual instinct has
been preponderantly autoerotic; it now finds the sexual object. Thus far, it has manifested itself in single impulses and
in erogenous zones seeking a certain pleasure as a single
sexual aim. A new sexual aim now appears for the production of which all partial impulses cooperate, while the
erogenous zones subordinate themselves to the primacy of
the genital zone. As the new sexual aim assigns very different functions to the two sexes, their sexual developments
now part company. The male sexual development is more
consistent and easier to understand, while in the woman a
sort of regression seems to appear. The normality of the sexual life is guaranteed only by the exact concurrence of the
two streams directed to the sexual object and sexual aim. It
is like the piercing of a tunnel from opposite sides.

The new sexual aim in the man consists in the discharge
of the sexual products. This is not contradictory to the former sexual aim, which is that of obtaining pleasure; on the

contrary, the height of all pleasure is connected with this final act in the sexual process. The sexual instinct now enters into the service of the function of propagation; it becomes, so to say, altruistic. If this transformation is to succeed, its process must be adjusted to the original dispositions and all the peculiarities of the impulses.

TCTS III

Let us finally add that during the transition period of puberty the somatic and psychic processes of development proceed side by side, but separately, until with the breaking through of an intense psychic love-stimulus for the innervation of the genitals, the normally demanded unification of the erotic function is established.

TCTS III

SHAME—The age of childhood, in which the sense of shame is unknown, seems a paradise when we look back upon it later, and paradise itself is nothing but the mass-phantasy of the childhood of the individual. This is why in paradise men are naked and unashamed, until the moment arrives when shame and fear awaken; expulsion follows, and sexual life and cultural development begin. Into this paradise dreams can take us back every night; we have already ventured the conjecture that the impressions of our earliest childhood (from the prehistoric period until about the end of the third year) crave reproduction for their own sake, perhaps without further reference to their content, so that their repetition is a wish-fulfilment. Dreams of nakedness, then, are *exhibition-dreams.*

IoD—ch. 5

SLEEP—The necessary mental pre-condition of sleep is the concentration of the ego upon the wish to sleep and the withdrawal of psychical energy from all the interests of life;

since at the same time all the paths of approach to motility are blocked, the ego is also able to reduce the expenditure of energy by which at other times it maintains the repressions.
ABS—ch. 4

The state of sleep makes dream-formation possible by reducing the endopsychic censorship.
IoD—ch. 7

The thought-impulses continued into sleep may be divided into the following groups:
1. Those which have not been completed during the day, owing to some accidental cause.
2. Those which have been left uncompleted because our mental powers have failed us, i.e. unsolved problems.
3. Those which have been turned back and suppressed during the day. This is reinforced by a powerful fourth group:
4. Those which have been excited in our *Ucs.* during the day by the workings of the *Pcs;* and finally we may add a fifth, consisting of:
5. The indifferent impressions of the day, which have therefore been left unsettled.
IoD—ch. 7

The state of sleep represents a turning away from the real external world, and thus provides a necessary condition for the development of a psychosis.
NILP—ch. 1

The fact of dream-censorship shows that enough repressive resistance remains operative even during sleep.
NILP—ch. 1

SPEECH—. . . . the function of speech . . . brings the material in the ego into a firm connection with the memory-traces of visual and more particularly of auditory perceptions.
OoPA—ch. 4

Speech in the Dream—When in a dream something has the character of a spoken utterance—that is, when it is said or heard, not merely thought—and the distinction can usually be made with certainty—then it originates in the utterances of waking life, which have, of course, been treated as raw material, dismembered, and slightly altered, and above all removed from their context.
IoD—ch. 5

SUBCONSCIOUS—When someone talks of the subconscious, I do not know whether he means it topographically, as what lies in the psyche below consciousness, or qualitatively, as another consciousness—a subterranean one as it were. Probably he is not clear on the point himself. The only admissible antithesis is between conscious and unconscious. But it would be a serious error to suppose that this distinction coincides with that between the Ego and the Id.
QLA—ch. 2

SUBLIMATION—Sublimation is a process that concerns the object-libido and consists in the instinct's directing itself towards an aim other than, and remote from, that of sexual gratification; in this process the accent falls upon the deflection from the sexual aim.
Narc

The process through which the excessive excitations from individual sexual sources are discharged and utilized in other spheres, so that no small enhancement of mental capacity results from a predisposition which is dangerous as such.
TCTS III

The tendency to repression, as well as the ability to sublimate, must be traced back to the organic bases of the character, upon which alone the psychic structure arises.
LDV—ch. 6

SUGGESTION   (SUGGESTIBILITY)—Suggestion   (or
more correctly suggestibility) is actually an irreducible,
primitive phenomenon, a fundamental fact in the mental
life of man.
GPAE—ch. 3
  What distinguishes a suggestion from other kinds of
mental influence, such as a command or the giving of a
piece of information or instruction, is that in the case of a
suggestion an idea is aroused in another person's brain
which is not examined in regard to its origin but is accepted
just as though it had arisen spontaneously in that brain.
H & S

SUICIDE—There are some neurotics in whom, to judge by
all their reactions, the instinct of self-preservation has actually been reversed. They seem to have nothing in view but
self-injury and self-destruction. It is possible that people
who in the end do in fact commit suicide belong to this
group.
OoPA—ch. 1

SUPEREGO—In the course of the individual development
a part of the inhibiting forces in the outer world becomes internalized; a standard is created in the Ego which opposes
the other faculties by observation, criticism, and prohibition. We call this new standard the Super-ego.
M & M—Part III, Section II
  The Superego is the successor and representative of the
parents (and educators) who superintended the actions of
the individual in his first years of life; it perpetuates their
functions almost without a change.
M & M—Part III, Section II
  When I set out the relationship of Ego and Id I kept back
an important part of the theory of the psychical apparatus.

It is this: we were forced to assumed that in the Ego itself a special agency has become differentiated, which we name the Super-Ego. This Super-Ego holds a special position between the Ego and the Id. It belongs to the Ego, shares its high psychological organization, but stands in an especially intimate connection with the Id. It is, actually, the precipitate of the Ego's first attachments to objects; the heir of the Œdipus complex, when that has been vacated. This Super-Ego can set itself against the Ego. It can treat it as an object, and often uses it very harshly. It is just as important for the Ego to live in concord with the Super-Ego as with the Id. Discords between Ego and Super-Ego have great significance for psychical life. You will have guessed by now that the Super-Ego is the vehicle for the phenomenon we call "conscience." It is very important for mental health that the Super-Ego should develop normally —that is, that it should become sufficiently depersonalized. It is precisely this that does not happen in the case of a neurotic, because his Œdipus complex does not undergo the right transformation. His Super-Ego deals with his Ego like a strict father with a child, and his idea of morality displays itself in primitive ways by making the Ego submit to punishment by the Super-Ego. Illness is employed as a means for this "self-punishment." The neurotic has to behave as though he were mastered by guilt, which the illness serves to punish, and so to relieve him.
QLA—ch 5

SUPERSTITION—The phenomena of superstition furnish another indication of the unconscious motivation in chance and faulty actions.
PEL—ch. 10

Because the superstitious person knows nothing of the motivation of his own accidental actions, and because the

fact of this motivation strives for a place in his recognition, he is compelled to dispose of them by displacing them into the outer world. As a matter of fact, I believe that a large portion of the mythological conception of the world which reaches far into the most modern religions, is *nothing but psychology projected to the outer world.*
PEL—ch. 10

SYMPTOM—The symptom has its origin in the repressed, it is as it were the representative of the repressed in relation to the ego; the repressed is a foreign territory to the ego, an internal foreign territory, just as reality is—you must excuse the unusual expression—an external foreign territory.
NILP—ch. 3

SYMPTOM AND CHANCE ACTION—Cases [of lapses of our motor function] in which the entire action appears rather inexpedient, I call "symptomatic and chance actions."
PEL—ch. 8

Symptom and the Ego—The process which through repression has become a symptom maintains its existence outside of the ego-organization and independent of it.
PoA—ch. 3

SYMPTOM-FORMATION—Symptoms result from the injuring of the instinctual impulse through repression.
PoA—ch. 2
  Symptoms are supposed to be an indication of and substitute for an unachieved instinctual gratification; they are, that is, a result of a process of repression.
PoA—ch. 2
  Symptom formation thus has the actual result of putting end to the danger situation.
PoA—ch. 9

All phenomena of symptom-formation can be fairly described as "the return of the repressed." The distinctive character of them, however, lies in the extensive distortion the returning elements have undergone, compared with their original form.
M & M—Part III, Section II

SYPHILOPHOBIA—Castration anxiety persists in the guise of syphilophobia, after it has been learned that castration is no longer customary as a punishment for giving the sexual appetites free rein but that serious diseases threaten instinctual freedom instead.
PoA—ch. 9

I may refer to the case of a young man who became agoraphobic because he was afraid of yielding to the allurements of prostitutes and of acquiring syphilis as a punishment.
PoA—ch. 7

SYSTEM—The secondary elaboration of the product of the dream-work is an excellent example of the nature and the pretensions of a system. An intellectual function in us demands the unification, coherence and comprehensibility of everything perceived and thought of, and does not hesitate to construct a false connection if, as a result of special circumstances, it cannot grasp the right one. We know such system formation not only from the dream, but also from phobias, from compulsive thinking and from the types of delusions. The system formation is most ingenious in delusional states (paranoia) and dominates the clinical picture, but it also must not be overlooked in other forms of neuropsychoses. In every case we can show that a rearrangement of the psychic material takes place, which may often be quite violent, provided it seems comprehensible from the point of view of the system. The best indication that a system has been formed then lies in the fact that each result of it can be shown to have at least two motivations, one of which springs from the assumptions of the system and is therefore eventually delusional—and a hidden one which, however, we must recognize as the real and effective motivation.

T & T—ch. 3

T

TABOO—Taboo is a Polynesian word, the translation of which provides difficulties for us because we no longer possess the idea which it connotes. It was still current with the ancient Romans: their word "sacer" was the same as the taboo of the Polynesians. The ἄγος of the Greeks and the Kodaush of the Hebrews must also have signified the same thing which the Polynesians express through their word taboo and what many races in America, Africa (Madagascar), North and Central Asia express through analogous designations.

For us the meaning of taboo branches off into two opposite directions. On the one hand it means to us, sacred, consecrated: but on the other hand it means, uncanny, dangerous, forbidden, and unclean. The opposite for taboo is designated in Polynesian by the word *noa* and signifies something ordinary and generally accessible. Thus something like the concept of reserve inheres in taboo; taboo expresses itself essentially in prohibitions and restrictions. Our combination of "holy dread" would often express the meaning of taboo.

T & T—ch. 2

Let us summarize what understanding we have gained

of taboo through its comparison with the compulsive prohibition of the neurotic. Taboo is a very primitive prohibition imposed from without (by an authority) and directed against the strongest desires of man. The desire to violate it continues in the unconscious; persons who obey the taboo have an ambivalent feeling toward what is affected by the taboo. The magic power attributed to taboo goes back to its ability to lead man into temptation; it behaves like a contagion, because the example is contagious, and because the prohibited desire becomes displaced in the unconscious upon something else. The expiation for the violation of a taboo through a renunciation proves that a renunciation is at the basis of the observance of the taboo.
T & T—ch. 2

Taboo and Compulsion Neurosis—He who approaches the problem of taboo from the field of psychoanalysis, which is concerned with the study of the unconscious part of the individual's psychic life, needs but a moment's reflection to realize that these phenomena are by no means foreign to him. He knows people who have individually created such taboo prohibitions for themselves, which they follow as strictly as savages observe the taboos common to their tribe or society. If he were not accustomed to call these individuals "compulsion neurotics" he would find the term "taboo disease" quite appropriate for their malady. Psychoanalytic investigation has taught him the clinical etiology and the essential part of the psychological mechanism of this compulsion disease, so that he cannot resist applying what he has learnt there to explain corresponding manifestations in folk psychology.

There is one warning to which we shall have to give heed in making this attempt. The similarity between taboo and compulsion disease may be purely superficial, holding

good only for the manifestations of both without extending
int^ their deeper characteristics. . . . The first and most
striking correspondence between the compulsion prohibitions of neurotics and taboo lies in the fact that the origin of
these prohibitions is just as unmotivated and enigmatic.
They have appeared at some time or other and must now be
retained on account of an unconquerable anxiety. An external threat of punishment is superfluous, because an inner
certainty (a conscience) exists that violation will be followed by unbearable disaster. The very most that compulsion patients can tell us is the vague premonition that some
person of their environment will suffer harm if they should
violate the prohibition. Of what the harm is to consist is not
known, and this inadequate information is more likely to be
obtained during the later discussions of the expiatory and
defensive actions than when the prohibitions themselves
are being discussed. . . . Compulsion prohibitions, like
taboo prohibitions, entail the most extraordinary renuncia-
tions and restrictions of life, but a part of these can be removed by carrying out certain acts which now also must be
done because they have acquired a compulsive character
(obsessive acts); there is no doubt that these acts are in the
nature of penances, expiations, defence reactions, and pu-
rifications. The most common of these obsessive acts is
washing with water (washing obsession). A part of the
taboo prohibitions can also be replaced in this way, that is to
say, their violation can be made good through such a "ceremonial," and here too lustration through water is the preferred way.

Let us now summarize the points in which the correspondence between taboo customs and the symptoms of
compulsion neurosis are most clearly manifested: 1. In the
lack of motivation of the commandments, 2. in their en-
forcement through an inner need, 3. in their capacity for

displacement and in the danger of contagion from what is prohibited, 4. and in the causation of ceremonial actions and commandments which emanate from the forbidden. T & T—ch. 2

Taboo and Touching—In its attempt to prevent associations from occurring, to obstruct the forming of connections in thought, the ego is complying with one of the oldest and most fundamental commandments of the compulsion neurosis, the taboo on touching. To the question why the avoidance of touching, contact or contagion plays so large a rôle in the neurosis and is made the content of so complicated a system, the answer is that touching, physical contact, is the most immediate aim of aggressive no less than of tender object-cathexes. Eros desires contact, for it strives for union, for the annihilation of spatial boundaries between ego and loved object. But destruction, too, which before the invention of long-range weapons could be effected only through proximity, necessarily presupposes physical contact, the use of the hands. To touch a woman has become in ordinary parlance a euphemism for her use as a sexual object. Not to touch the genital is the usual wording of the prohibition against autoerotic gratification. Since the compulsion neurosis sought to effect erotic contact in the first place, and then, subsequent to regression, the same contact disguised as aggression, nothing was taboo to it in such intense degree as this very contact, nothing was so fitted to become the keystone of a system of prohibitions.
PoA—ch. 6

TELEPATHY—You know that by telepathy we mean the alleged fact that an event which occurs at a specific time comes more or less simultaneously into the consciousness of a person who is spatially distant, without any of the

known methods of communication coming into play. The tacit assumption is that this event occurs to a person, in whom the receiver of the message has some strong emotional interest. . . . I need not emphasize to you the improbability of such processes, and anyway there are good reasons for rejecting the majority of such reports.
NILP—ch. 2

Have I given you the impression that I am secretly inclined to support the reality of telepathy in the occult sense? If so, I should very much regret that it is so difficult to avoid giving such an impression. In reality, however, I was anxious to be strictly impartial. I have every reason to be so, for I have no opinion; I know nothing about it.
D & T

Telepathy and Dream—Fundamentally the dream has but little to do with telepathy. Telepathy throws no new light on the nature of the dream, nor does the dream bear witness for the reality of telepathy. Telepathic phenomena are also by no manner of means confined to dreams; they can also manifest themselves during waking life. The only ground for mentioning the connection between dreams and telepathy is that the condition of sleep seems to be especially suitable for the reception of telepathic communications. If then one comes across a so-called telepathic dream, one can convince oneself by its analysis that the telepathic message has played the same rôle as any other residue of waking life, and as such has been altered by the dream-work and made to serve its purpose.

I want you to notice that it was not dreams that seemed to teach us something about telepathy, but the interpretation of the dreams, the psycho-analytic treatment of them.
NILP—ch. 2

THOUGHT-PROCESSES—Thought-processes, and what may be analogous to them in the Id, are unconscious *per se* and obtain their entry into consciousness by their connection, via the function of speech, with memory traces of perceptions through touch and ear.
M & M—Part III, Section I

THOUGHT-TRANSFERENCE—There is, for example, the phenomenon of thought-transference, which is closely allied to telepathy and, indeed, can be identified with it without much difficulty. It is held that psychological processes, ideas, states of excitement, volitions, which occur in the mind of one person, can be transferred through space to another, without the usual means of communication (words or signs) being employed. Incidentally it is remarkable that it is actually these phenomena which find the least mention in the old accounts of the miraculous.
NILP—ch. 2

TIME-PERCEPTION—The relation of time, too, which is so hard to describe, is communicated to the ego by the perceptual system; indeed it can hardly be doubted that the mode in which this system works is the source of the idea of time.
NILP—ch. 3

TOTEMISM—Among the Australians the system of *Totemism* takes the place of all religious and social institutions. Australian tribes are divided into smaller *septs* or clans, each taking the name of its *totem*. Now what is a totem? As a rule it is an animal, either edible or harmless, or dangerous and feared; more rarely the totem is a plant or a force of nature (rain, water), which stands in a peculiar relation to the whole clan. The totem is first of all the tribal an-

cestor of the clan, as well as its tutelary spirit and protector; it sends oracles and, though otherwise dangerous, the totem knows and spares its children. The members of a totem are therefore under a sacred obligation not to kill (destroy) their totem, to abstain from eating its meat or from any other enjoyment of it. Any violation of these prohibitions is automatically punished. The character of a totem is inherent not only in a single animal or a single being but in all the members of the species. From time to time festivals are held at which the members of a totem represent or imitate, in ceremonial dances, the movements and characteristics of their totems. . . . We must consider that peculiarity of the totemic system which attracts the interest of the psychoanalyst. Almost everywhere where the totem prevails, there also exists the law that *the members of the same totem are not allowed to enter into sexual relations with each other; that is, that they cannot marry each other.* This represents the *exogamy* which is associated with the totem.
T & T—ch. 1

Totemism as the Earliest Religion—Totemism, with its worship of a father substitute, the ambivalency towards the father which is evidenced by the totem feast, the institution of remembrance festivals and of laws the breaking of which is punished by death—this totemism, I conclude, may be regarded as the earliest appearance of religion in the history of mankind, and it illustrates the close connection existing from the very beginning of time between social institutions and moral obligations.
M & M—Part III, Section I

Though it may seem that instinctual renunciation, and the ethics based on it, do not belong to the essence of religion, still they are genetically closely related to religion. Totemism, the first form of religion of which we know, con-

tains as an indispensable part of its system a number of
laws and prohibitions which plainly mean nothing else but
instinctual renunciation.
M & M—Part III, Section II

TRANSFERENCE (IN ANALYSIS)—The patient sees in
his analyst the return—the reincarnation—of some important figure out of his childhood or past, and consequently
transfers on to him feelings and reactions that undoubtedly
applied to this model. It soon becomes evident that this fact
of transference is a factor of undreamed-of importance—on
the one hand an instrument of irreplaceable value and on
the other a source of serious dangers. This transference is
ambivalent: it comprises positive and affectionate as well as
negative and hostile attitudes toward the analyst, who, as a
rule, is put in the place of one or other of the patient's parents, his father or his mother. So long as it is positive it
serves us admirably. It alters the whole analytic situation
and sidetracks the patient's rational aim of becoming well
and free from his troubles. Instead of it there emerges the
aim of pleasing the analyst, of winning his applause and his
love. This becomes the true motive-force for the patient's
collaboration; the weak ego becomes strong; under the influence of this aim the patient achieves things that would
otherwise be beyond his power; his symptoms disappear
and he seems to have recovered—all of this simply out of
love for his analyst. . . . Therapeutic successes that take
place under the sway of the positive transference are under
the suspicion of being of a *suggestive* nature. If the negative
transference gains the upper hand they are blown away like
spray before the wind. [See also *Analyst, Personal Influence
of.*]
OoPA—ch. 6

TRAUMA (PSYCHIC)—In traumatic neurosis the active cause of illness is not the trifling bodily injury but the affect of fright—the psychic trauma. Similarly, our investigations of many, if not of the majority, of hysterical symptoms have revealed causes which must be described as psychic traumas.

PMHP—ch. 1

The impressions we experienced at an early age and forgot later, to which I have ascribed such great importance for the ætiology of the neuroses, are called traumata.

M & M—Part III, Section I

U

UNCONSCIOUS—The oldest and best meaning of the word "unconscious" is the descriptive one; we call "unconscious" any mental process the existence of which we are obliged to assume—because, for instance, we infer it in some way from its effects—but of which we are not directly aware. . . . If we want to be more accurate, we should modify the statement by saying that we call a process "unconscious" when we have to assume that it was active *at a certain time,* although *at that time* we knew nothing about it. NILP—ch. 3

Certainly, large portions of the ego and super-ego can remain unconscious, are, in fact, normally unconscious. That means to say that the individual knows nothing of their contents and that it requires an expenditure of effort to make him conscious of them. It is true, then, that ego and conscious, repressed and unconscious do not coincide. NILP—ch. 3

Unconscious and Preconscious—There are *two kinds of unconscious,* which have not as yet been distinguished by psychologists. Both are unconscious in the psychological sense; but in our sense the first, which we call *Ucs.,* is likewise

incapable of *consciousness;* whereas the second we call *Pcs.* because its excitations, after the observance of certain rules, are capable of reaching consciousness; perhaps not before they have again undergone censorship, but nevertheless regardless of the *Ucs. system.* The fact that in order to attain consciousness the excitations must pass through an unalterable series, a succession of instances, as is betrayed by the changes produced in them by the censorship, has enabled us to describe them by analogy in spatial terms. We described the relations of the two systems to each other and to consciousness by saying that the system *Pcs.* is like a screen between the system *Ucs.* and consciousness. The system *Pcs.* not only bars access to consciousness, but also controls the access to voluntary motility, and has control of the emission of a mobile cathectic energy, a portion of which is familiar to us as attention.
IoD—ch. 7

UNCONSCIOUS MENTAL PROCESSES, TIMELESS-NESS OF—We have found by experience that unconscious mental processes are in themselves "timeless." That is to say to begin with: they are not arranged chronologically, time alters nothing in them, nor can the idea of time be applied to them.
BPP—ch. 4

UNDOING—It is a kind of negative magic which by means of a motor symbolism would "blow away," as it were, not the consequences of an event (an impression, an experience), but the event itself. . . . The effort at "undoing" finds its reflection in the normal sphere in the resolve to treat an occurrence as *non arrivé;* but in this case one does not take up arms against it, one is simply not concerned about either the occurrence or its consequences; whereas in neurosis the attempt is made to abrogate the past itself, to repress it by motor means. An effort of the same sort may provide the explanation of the compulsion to *repetition* so frequently present in neurosis, a repetition in the carrying out of which various mutually contradictory purposes are commingled. . . . The striving to "undo" a traumatic experience is often revealed as a motive force of the first rank in the creating of symptoms.

PoA—ch. 6

V

VERBAL IMAGE—The part played by verbal images becomes perfectly clear. By their interposition internal thought-processes are made into perceptions.
E & I—ch. 2

VOMITING—As an hysterical defense against eating, the symptom of vomiting is familiar.
PoA—ch. 1

W

WALKING—Locomotion is inhibited in many neurotic states by antipathy to walking and weakness in walking; the hysterical disability makes use of paralysis of the motor apparatus or creates a specific suspension of this one function of the latter (abasia). Particularly characteristic are the difficulties of locomotion brought about by the interpolation of definite conditions as prerequisites, the non-fulfillment of which evokes anxiety (phobia). . . . If walking has become a symbolic substitute for stamping on the body of Mother Earth, then . . . walking will be abstained from, because it is as though forbidden sexual behavior were thereby indulged in.
PoA—ch. 1

WAR—Anything that encourages the growth of emotional ties between men must operate against war.
WW

WAR NEUROSES—The war neuroses, in so far as they are distinguished from the ordinary neuroses of peace-time by special characteristics, are to be regarded as traumatic neu-

roses whose occurrence has been made possible or has been promoted by a conflict in the ego.
PAWN

WEANING—It is probable that the fear of poisoning is connected with weaning. Poison is the nourishment that makes one ill. Perhaps, moreover, the child traces his early illnesses back to this frustration.
NILP—ch. 5

WELTANSCHAUUNG—*"Weltanschauung"* is, I am afraid, a specifically German notion, which it would be difficult to translate into a foreign language. If I attempt to give you a definition of the word, it can hardly fail to strike you as inept. By *Weltanschauung*, then, I mean an intellectual construction, which gives a unified solution of all the problems of our existence in virtue of a comprehensive hypothesis, a construction, therefore, in which no question is left open and in which everything in which we are interested finds a place. It is easy to see that the possession of such a *Weltanschauung* is one of the ideal wishes of mankind. When one believes in such a thing, one feels secure in life, one knows what one ought to strive after, and how one ought to organise one's emotions and interests to the best purpose.
NILP—ch. 7

WISH-FULFILLMENT (IN DREAMS)—We assert that the dream is a wish-fulfilment; in order to take objections into account, you may say that the dream is an *attempted* wish-fulfilment. [See also *Dream and Wish-Fulfillment.*]
NILP—ch. 1

WIT—Wit is, so to speak, the contribution to the comic from the sphere of the unconscious.
WRU—ch. VII

Though wit-making is an excellent means of obtaining pleasure from the psychic processes, we know that not all persons are equally able to make use of it. Wit-making is not at the disposal of all, in general there are but a few persons to whom one can point and say that they are witty. Here wit seems to be a special ability somewhere within the region of the old "psychic faculties," and this shows itself in its appearance as fairly independent of the other faculties such as intelligence, phantasy, memory, etc. A special talent or psychic determination permitting or favoring wit-making must be presupposed in all wit-makers.
WRU—ch. V

WOMAN—. . . the female sex, the sex certainly more predisposed to neurosis. . . . It is precisely in the female that object loss seems to remain the most effective situation of danger. . . . Since it is certainly true that hysteria has a greater affinity with femininity, just as compulsion neurosis has with masculinity, the idea suggests itself that, as a determinant of anxiety, loss of love plays a rôle in hysteria similar to that of the threat of castration in the phobias and of dread of the superego in compulsion neurosis.
PoA—ch. 8

We attribute to women a greater amount of narcissism (and this influences their object-choice) so that for them to be loved is a stronger need than to love. Their vanity is partly a further effect of penis-envy, for they are driven to rate their physical charms more highly as a belated compensation for their original sexual inferiority. Modesty, which is regarded as a feminine characteristic *par excellence,*

but is far more a matter of convention than one would think, was, in our opinion, originally designed to hide the deficiency in her genitals.
NILP—ch. 5

WORDS [cf. also SPEECH; VERBAL IMAGE]—We do not, indeed, wish to decry *words*. They are a mighty instrument, the means by which we convey our feelings, the way by which we influence others. Words can do unutterable good, and appalling harm. No doubt, in the beginning was the deed—the word came later; in some contexts it was a cultural advance when deeds were moderated to words. But still, words were originally spells, acts of magic, and they still retain much of their old power.
QLA—ch. 1

WORK—The great majority work only when forced by necessity, and this natural human aversion to work gives rise to the most difficult social problems.
C & D—ch. 2

WORKING-OVER—We know that the anxiety of the neuroses can be relieved by further mental "working-over," *e.g.* by conversion, reaction-formation or defence-formation (phobia).
Narc

WRITING—If writing—which consists in allowing a fluid to flow out from a tube upon a piece of white paper—has acquired the symbolic meaning of coitus . . . then writing will be abstained from, because it is as though forbidden sexual behavior were thereby being indulged in.
PoA—ch. 1

Z

ZOOPHOBIA, INFANTILE—The relation of the child to animals has much in common with that of primitive man. The child does not yet show any trace of the pride which afterwards moves the adult civilized man to set a sharp dividing line between his own nature and that of all other animals. The child unhesitatingly attributes full equality to animals; he probably feels himself more closely related to the animal than to the undoubtedly mysterious adult, in the freedom with which he acknowledges his needs.

KEY TO REFERENCES

ABS—*An Autobiographical Study.*

A-N—*The Justification for Detaching from Neurasthenia a Particular Syndrome: The Anxiety-Neurosis. (Collected Papers, Vol. I)*

AnDS—*Some Psychological Consequences of the Anatomical Distinction between the Sexes. (Collected Papers, Vol. V)*

APF—*The Acquisition of Power over Fire. (Collected Papers, Vol. V)*

AP5B—*Analysis of a Phobia in a Five-Year-Old Boy. (Collected Papers, Vol. III)*

ASPW—*The Antithetical Sense of Primal Words. (Collected Papers, Vol. IV)*

AT & I—*Analysis, Terminable and Interminable. (Collected Papers, Vol. V)*

BPP—*Beyond the Pleasure Principle.*

C & AE—*Character and Anal Erotism. (Collected Papers, Vol. II)*

C & D—*Civilization and Its Discontents.*

CPL-DEL—*Contributions to the Psychology of Love. The Most Prevalent Form of Degradation in Erotic Life. (Collected Papers, Vol. IV)*

CPL-TV—*Contributions to the Psychology of Love. The Taboo of Virginity. (Collected Papers, Vol. IV)*

C-S&E—*A Connection between a Symbol and a Symptom. (Collected Papers, Vol. II)*

CSMN—*"Civilized" Sexual Morality and Modern Nervousness. (Collected Papers, Vol. II)*

CSOHP—*Some Points in a Comparative Study of Organic and Hysterical Paralysis. (Collected Papers, Vol. I)*

DNP—*The Defence of Neuro-Psychoses. (Collected Papers, Vol. I)*

D & T—*Dreams and Telepathy. (Collected Papers, Vol. IV)*

E & I—*The Ego and the Id.*

EPM—*The Economic Problem in Masochism. (Collected Papers, Vol. II)*

Fet—*Fetishism. (Collected Papers, Vol. V)*

FPMF—*Formulations regarding the two Principles in Mental Functioning. (Collected Papers, Vol. IV)*

FPT—*The Future Prospects of Psycho-Analytic Therapy. (Collected Papers, Vol. II)*

FRDNP—*Further Remarks on the Defence Psycho-Neuroses. (Collected Papers, Vol. I)*

FS—*Female Sexuality. (Collected Papers, Vol. V)*

GPAE—*Group Psychology and the Analysis of the Ego.*

GRHA—*General Remarks on Hysterical Attacks. (Collected Papers, Vol. II)*

HAN—*Heredity and the Aetiology of the Neuroses. (Collected Papers, Vol. I)*

HIF—*From the History of an Infantile Neurosis. (Collected Papers, Vol. III)*

H & S—*Hypnotism and Suggestion. (Collected Papers, Vol. V)*

Hum—*Humour. (Collected Papers, Vol. V)*

IoD—*The Interpretation of Dreams.*

I & V—*Instincts and their Vicissitudes. (Collected Papers, Vol. IV)*

IML—*Infantile Mental Life. (Collected Papers, Vol. I)*

LDV—*Leonardo da Vinci.*

LT—*The Libido Theory. (Collected Papers, Vol. V)*

M & M—*Moses and Monotheism.*

MSTD—*Metapsychological Supplement to the Theory of Dreams. (Collected Papers, Vol. IV)*

Narc—*On Narcissism: an Introduction. (Collected Papers, Vol. IV)*

Neg—*Negation. (Collected Papers, Vol. V)*

NILP—*New Introductory Lectures on Psychoanalysis.*

NM-JPH—*Certain Neurotic Mechanisms in Jealousy. Paranoia and Homosexuality. (Collected Papers, Vol. II)*

N & P—*Neurosis and Psychosis. (Collected Papers, Vol. II)*

OA & RL—*Obsessive Acts end Religious Practices. (Collected Papers, Vol. II)*

OoPA—*An Outline of Psychoanalysis.*

O & P—*Obsessions and Phobias; their Psychical Mechanisms and their Aetiology. (Collected Papers, Vol. I)*

OSD—*The Occult Significance of Dreams. (Collected Papers, Vol. V)*

PA—*Psycho-Analysis. (Collected Papers, Vol. V)*

PA & CL—*Psycho-Analysis and the Ascertaining of Truth in Courts of Law. (Collected Papers, Vol. II)*

ParDP—*Psycho-Analytic Notes upon an Autobiographical Account of a Case of Paranoia (Dementia Paranoides). (Collected Papers, Vol. III)*

PEL—*Psychopathology of Everyday Life.*

PMHP—*On the Psychical Mechanism of Hysterical Phenomena. (Collected Papers, Vol. I)*

PoA—*The Problem of Anxiety.*

PON—*The Predisposition to Obsessional Neurosis. (Collected Papers, Vol. II)*

PT—*On Psychotherapy. (Collected Papers, Vol. I)*

PVD—*Psychogenic Visual Disturbance according to Psycho-Analytical Conceptions. (Collected Papers, Vol. II)*

QLA—*The Question of Lay Analysis.*

RCA-N—*A Reply to Criticisms on the Anxiety-Neurosis. (Collected Papers, Vol. I)*

Repr—*Repression. (Collected Papers, Vol. IV)*

RPDD—*The Relation of the Poet to Day-Dreaming. (Collected Papers, Vol. IV)*

SAoN—*Sexuality in the Aetiology of Neuroses. (Collected Papers, Vol. I)*

SECh—*The Sexual Enlightenment of Children. (Collected Papers, Vol. II)*

SM—*Screen Memories. (Collected Papers, Vol. V)*

TCTS—*Three Contributions to the Theory of Sex.*

THA—*On the Theory of Hysterical Attacks. (Collected Papers, Vol. V)*

TIAE—*On the Transformation of Instincts with Special Reference to Anal Erotism. (Collected Papers, Vol. II)*

TNN—*Types of Neurotic Nosogenesis. (Collected Papers, Vol. II)*

TPDI—*Remarks upon the Theory and Practice of Dream-Interpretation. (Collected Papers, Vol. V)*

T & T—*Totem and Taboo.*

TTWD—*Thoughts for the Times on War and Death. (Collected Papers, Vol. IV)*

Uncanny—*The "Uncanny". (Collected Papers, Vol. IV)*

Ucs—*The Unconscious. (Collected Papers, Vol. IV)*

WRU—*Wit and Its Relation to the Unconscious.*

WW—*Why War? (Collected Papers, Vol. V)*